W9-DES-433

NEVER, NEVER GIVE UP

Jack Hartman

Dedication

To Ralph Mann, President of the Mission Possible Foundation. God has honored Ralph's perseverance and faithfulness with bountiful fruit in Eastern Bloc countries in Europe. Thank you, Ralph, for never giving up.

Copyright 1994 Jack Hartman
All rights reserved. Printed in the U.S.A.

No part of this book may be used or reproduced in
any manner whatsoever without written permission from
the publisher except in the case of brief quotations and
articles of review. For information on this book, please
write to:

Lamplight Ministries, Inc.
P.O. Box 1307
Dunedin, Florida 34697

Library of Congress Catalog Number: 94-96643
ISBN 0-915445-16-6

All Scripture quotations, unless otherwise indicated, are taken from *The Amplified Bible, Old Testament*, copyright 1965, 1987 by the Zondervan Corporation or *The Amplified Bible, New Testament*, copyright 1958, 1987 by the Lockman Corporation. Used by permission.

All Scripture references in this book are from *The Amplified Bible*. I first started using this version of the Bible when it was only available as a New Testament. I bought a paperback version of *The Amplified New Testament* because it said on the cover, "...the best study Testament on the market. It is a magnificent translation. I use it continually." (Dr. Billy Graham).

As I read about the origin of this version of the Bible, I found that a group of qualified Hebrew and Greek scholars spent a total of more than 20,000 hours on this project. They believed traditional word-by-word translations often fail to reveal the shades of meaning which are part of the Hebrew and Greek words.

After twenty years of extensive Bible study, I have found that *The Amplified Bible* reveals many spiritual truths that I can't find in other versions of the Bible. Because of this, I now use this version of the Bible in all of my books. I have added italics in some passages of Scripture to accentuate points I wish to emphasize.

If you aren't used to this translation of this Bible, please be patient with the brackets and parentheses. They are used to indicate what has been added in the amplification. I believe you'll find that *The Amplified Bible* contains a great deal of additional information that will help you to increase your patience and perseverance.

Table of Contents

Introduction

Sir Winston Churchill was sixty-six years old when he first became Prime Minister of Great Britain. In spite of his age, Mr. Churchill did an outstanding job during World War II. He refused to give up in the face of seemingly impossible problems. His tenacity and perseverance were an inspiration to millions of people all over the world.

Several years after Mr. Churchill retired as prime minister, he was asked to give the commencement address at Harrow, the school he had attended as a boy. Sir Winston hadn't spoken in public for many years. He had become a virtual recluse. When he agreed to speak to the graduating class, the English people awaited this rare public appearance with great anticipation.

Many members of the news media attended the commencement ceremonies. The headmaster of the school urged the students to take careful notes on the prime minister's speech. These young people were very excited about the opportunity to hear this famous man. The air was filled with anticipation just before the prime minister began to speak.

Mr. Churchill was quite feeble. He walked with a cane. After a long and flowery introduction, the prime minister walked slowly to the podium. When he finally arrived, he laid down his cane. For what seemed like a very long time, he stood at the podium saying nothing. For several minutes he made eye contact with row after row of people.

Finally, Mr. Churchill ended the prolonged period of silence. He summoned up the little strength he had remaining to give the shortest commencement speech ever given. He said, *"Never, never, never, never, never, never give up!*" He then turned away from the podium and returned to his seat.

The audience was stunned by the brevity of Mr. Churchill's remarks. They had expected to hear a long, eloquent speech. They couldn't believe these few words were his entire address. However, as the people in the audience reflected upon the meaning of the few words he said, loud applause started at one corner of the room. It spread throughout the audience. Everyone then rose to give Mr. Churchill a standing ovation. His speech was eloquent in its brevity.

The subject of this commencement speech is the subject of this book. *We must not give up!* I'll refer continually to three different words in this book – *patience, endurance* and *perseverance.* In the Bible, the words patience and endurance often are used interchangeably. I won't attempt to differentiate between them. Perseverance is similar to patience and endurance. I'll explain exactly what perseverance is and how it differs from patient endurance.

A patient person is someone who is able to deal with any frustrating person, problem or situation with tolerance, calmness and self-control. Patient people are even tempered. They refuse to become frustrated, provoked or angered. Patient people are consistent in their response to problems.

The first five chapters of this book deal with the subject of patience. I'll explain the relationship between faith and patience. I'll give several examples to show why I believe our generation is more impatient than any generation in history. We'll look into the Word of God to study several scriptural examples of patience. We'll examine the difference between God's timing and our timing. I'll explain why Satan wants us to hurry and rush. We'll see that our Father doesn't want us to hurry.

The remaining chapters cover the subject of perseverance. Persevering people are goal-oriented, single-minded and unceasing. They are doggedly determined. They refused to be denied no matter what obstacles they face. Persevering people have great stamina. They are able to keep going in the face of severe opposition. They refuse to give up.

It is possible to be a patient person without being a persevering person. It also is possible for a persistent person to be an impatient person. Some people are born with a calm, easygoing temperament. It's very natural for these people to be patient, but some of these people don't do a good job of persevering in the face of extreme pressure.

Other people have an intense, high strung temperament from birth. These people usually find it difficult to be patient. However, some of the most persevering people are impatient people who are hard driving and intense.

This book is designed to help us become *both* patient and persevering. In addition to the five chapters I've written about patience, I also have written thirteen chapters on the subject of perseverance. We'll study dozens of specific instructions on perseverance from the Word of God. This book also contains some inspiring stories of people who have succeeded because they persevered.

We'll learn how to appropriate the strength and ability of Almighty God to persevere when human strength and ability are insufficient. I'll explain what it means to wait on the Lord. We'll see how the Word of God instructs us to build ourselves up spiritually while we're waiting for our Father to answer our prayers.

I'll explain how to get up when we're knocked down. We'll study God's Word to see what it says about perseverance and prayer. Finally, we'll look into the holy

Scriptures to see what they say about the blessings our Father provides for His children who persevere in faith.

Before I write a book, I usually study other Christian books to see what has been written on the subject I want to write about. I was surprised to find that very little seems to have been written about patience, endurance and perseverance.

Because you are reading this book, you must want to learn more about these subjects. I'd like to start by asking how many Scripture references you know pertaining to these subjects. When I taught classes on this subject, I found that many people in the class *didn't know any* Scripture references pertaining to patience, endurance and perseverance. Very few people knew as many as *ten* Scripture references. This book contains *almost three hundred Scripture references* on patience, endurance and perseverance.

I can tell you from personal experience that continual study and meditation on these Scripture references has helped me to become much more patient and persevering. I *didn't* write this book because I have been gifted with patience since birth. Instead, as I realized *how impatient I was*, I became very determined to study God's Word to learn everything I could about patience, endurance and perseverance. I learned a lot and my patience, endurance and perseverance improved.

I have used more italics in this book than in any other book I have written. I did this because I want to place the same emphasis on what I write that I do when I speak. I have taught almost eight hundred Bible study classes and I always emphasize the words I believe are important when I teach.

I spoke the first drafts of this book into a dictaphone. I also taught from the manuscript of this book in my church.

I have had ample opportunity to emphasize the contents of this book verbally and I have tried to carry this emphasis from the spoken word over to the written word. I have a burning desire to give the readers of my books as much information as I possibly can to help them bring the victory of Jesus Christ into manifestation in their lives. I pray that the contents of this book will be a blessing to you.

Chapter 1

We Must Add Patience
to Our Faith

The Bible has a great deal to say about the importance of faith. Faith *is* important, but we often have to *add patient endurance* to our faith to receive manifestation of the promises in the Word of God. The Bible speaks of "...those who *through faith* (by their leaning of the entire personality on God in Christ in absolute trust and confidence in His power, wisdom, and goodness) *and by practice of patient endurance and waiting are [now] inheriting the promises*" (Hebrews 6:12).

I like the way the amplification of the original Greek describes faith as the "leaning of the entire personality on God in Christ in absolute trust and confidence in His power, wisdom, and goodness." When we face seemingly unsolvable problems, our Father wants us to *lean* on Him. He wants us to *trust* in His power, wisdom and goodness with complete confidence. If we want to inherit the promises in God's Word, we often must *endure patiently* while we wait for our Father to bring His promises into manifestation.

Some Christians fail to add patience to their faith. It isn't uncommon for Christians to exhibit strong faith for awhile and then to give up because God hasn't answered their prayers. They say something like, "This 'faith stuff' doesn't work. I've been waiting two whole weeks and God still hasn't answered."

God *is* faithful to the promises in His Word. He is *completely dependable*. However, we must do our part. Our Father looks for *"...the steadfastness of the saints* [the patience, the endurance of the people of God], those who [habitually] keep God's commandments and [their] faith in Jesus" (Revelation 14:12).

Our Father wants us to be *steadfast*. This word is made up of two parts — "stead" and "fast." The word "stead" can be expanded into the word "steady" which means firm, consistent and unwavering. The word "fast" in this context means something that cannot be easily moved.

We often are required to add steadfastness to our faith. The apostle Paul commended the Thessalonians *"...for your steadfastness* (your unflinching endurance and patience) and your *firm faith* in the midst of all the persecutions and crushing distresses and afflictions under which you are holding up" (II Thessalonians 1:4).

The Thessalonians were able to persevere because they were steadfast. The amplification defines steadfastness as "unflinching endurance and patience." If we flinch, we bend and draw back. Our Father doesn't want us to flinch. When we face difficult problems, He wants us to react with *steadfastness* and *firm faith*.

In the first part of this chapter, I gave you the definition of faith from *The Amplified Bible*. Now let's look at the amplification of the original Greek to see what patience is. *"...patience [which is tireless and long-suffering, and has the power to endure whatever comes, with good temper]"* (Colossians 3:12).

We need to be *tireless* so we won't become weary when we face a prolonged season of adversity. We need

15

to tap into the power of God so we'll be able to endure whatever we're called upon to face. Instead of complaining, we should endure our problems *with good temper.*

We can only follow these instructions if we have the ability to control our emotions during difficult times. God's Word says that *self-control* is the key to patience. We're instructed to "...[develop] *self-control*, and in [exercising] *self-control* [develop] steadfastness (patience, endurance) ..." (II Peter 1:6).

Some people become discouraged if they can't see an answer to their problems. Our Father doesn't want us to give up hope. If we can't see an answer, He wants us to wait patiently for it. "...if we hope for what is *still unseen* by us, *we wait for it with patience and composure*" (Romans 8:25).

While we're waiting for our Father to do what His Word says He will do, *we must not allow our emotions to control us.* Our emotions are part of our souls which consist of our minds, our emotions and our will. Jesus told us how to control our souls. He said, *"By your steadfastness and patient endurance you shall win the true life of your souls"* (Luke 21:19).

Satan attempts to get at us *through our souls.* He wants to control our *minds* and *emotions.* He wants us to make *wrong decisions* under pressure. We must learn to control our souls. Our Father often withholds the blessings He promises in His Word until we exhibit *both* faith and patience. "Better is the *end* of a thing than the beginning of it, and the *patient in spirit is better than the proud in spirit*" (Ecclesiastes 7:8).

Pride and impatience go together. When self-centered people don't receive immediate results, they often attempt to take matters into their own hands. They try to make things happen because they believe everything revolves around them.

Our Father wants His children to be humble and trusting. *Humility and patience go together.* Proud, self-centered people seldom receive manifestation of the promises in God's Word. We must be patient. Our Father usually bestows His blessings at the *end* of a problem instead of at the beginning.

Our Father wants us to *let go* of our problems and give them to Him. We must learn to do more than just give our problems to God. *We must learn to leave them with Him.* "Casting the *whole of your care [all* your anxieties, *all* your worries, *all* your concerns, *once and for all]* on Him, for He cares for you affectionately and cares about you watchfully" (I Peter 5:7).

This passage of Scripture is one of my favorites. Our Father wants us to *cast all of our anxieties, worries and concerns on Him.* When we cast something, we throw it with great force. Our Father doesn't want us to hang onto problems. He wants us to *throw them to Him.*

Please notice the italicized word *whole,* the four times the word *all* is used in this Scripture and the words *once and for all.* Our Father wants us to give Him the *whole* of our problems. He wants us to give *all* of our anxieties, worries and concerns to Him.

God wants us to patiently leave our problems with Him *once and for all.* We must wait for His answer *for as long as He requires.* Our Father loves us more than we can comprehend. He watches each of His children carefully. He knows exactly what we're going through.

If we really trust our Father, *we won't place any time limit on our trust in Him.* We'll trust Him as long as He wants us to wait. We shouldn't be surprised if His answer takes longer than we believe it should. "Cast your bread upon the waters, for you will find it *after many days*" (Ecclesiastes 11:1).

When this passage of Scripture was written, the Egyptians often cast seeds upon the waters of a river. They knew the river would eventually carry their seeds into fertile mud that would produce a fine harvest. They realized that it would take a long time to receive the harvest and they weren't surprised by the delay.

Our Father wants us to apply these same principles today. When we sow seeds of faith, we are similar to farmers. When a farmer sows seeds into the ground, he doesn't expect an immediate harvest. Jesus said, "...The kingdom of God is like a man who scatters seed upon the ground, and then *continues sleeping and rising night and day* while the seed sprouts and grows and increases — *he knows not how*" (Mark 4:26-27).

Most farmers don't understand everything that takes place under the soil. They know that seeds that are properly planted and cultivated will produce a harvest. While they wait for this harvest, many days go by. They get up in the morning, do their chores and go to sleep at night. While the days are passing, the seeds are sprouting, growing and increasing until they produce a harvest.

The Word of God compares our need for patience with the patience exhibited by farmers. "...See how the farmer *waits expectantly* for the precious harvest from the land. [See how] he *keeps up* his patient [vigil] over it *until it receives* the early and late rains. *So you also must be patient...*" (James 5:7-8).

When we pray with faith, *we plant spiritual seeds*. Even though we can't see these seeds of faith taking root and preparing to produce a harvest, we must not give up.

Farmers in Bible times tried to plant seeds so the early rain would fall shortly after the seeds had been put into the ground. This early rain helped the seeds to germinate. Then, the farmers continued to wait until the latter rain came. They tried to plant their crops so this rain would come just before the time of harvest. The latter rain causes crops to ripen.

Farmers can't produce an income until they harvest their crops. If their bills are overdue and they need funds badly, they must want to rush the harvest, but they *know* they *can't* do this. *Farmers must wait patiently until the Lord gives them a harvest.* We also must wait patiently until the Lord gives us the answer we are waiting for.

In this first chapter, we have looked at twelve Scripture references to see *why* our Father wants us to be patient. Now that we've established this foundation from God's Word, let's look carefully at the environment we live in today to see the relationship between our lifestyle and our ability to be patient.

Chapter 2

Our Impatient Generation

This book contains eighteen chapters. Seventeen chapters are positive and uplifting. This chapter is the one exception. Please bear with me. I include the material in this chapter only to explain why I believe it is much more difficult to be patient today than it was when our great-grandparents lived.

I believe the people living in the United States at this time are *the most impatient group of people in history.* Our lifestyle tends to cause us to be impatient. People from foreign countries who visit the United States often are amazed at the fast pace of our lives. Most Americans have lived so long in this environment that our pace of living seems natural to us.

Several years ago, a Christian businessman from New Zealand visited me. When I drove him from the airport to our home, he was amazed at the high speed of the automobiles on the turnpike. I was driving at the speed limit, but automobiles continually passed us as if we were standing still. He was very surprised to see so many people driving so rapidly.

Have you ever driven at or near the speed limit only to have several automobiles speed past you? Haven't you observed many drivers who impatiently change from one lane to another just to get one or two car lengths ahead in heavy traffic?

A study of automobile accidents in the county where I live showed a significant increase in accidents during recent years. This increase was caused primarily by drivers running into automobiles in front of them that had stopped for a traffic light. Apparently the drivers in the following automobiles had assumed that the cars ahead of them would keep going even though the traffic light had turned yellow or red.

Many younger drivers are extremely impatient. We often hear the squeal of their tires as they try to get off to a fast start. Some young people race their motors while they wait at traffic lights. The loud music on their radios and tape players contributes to their impatience.

We usually see an example of impatience whenever there is a traffic delay. Sometimes people honk their horns when the automobile in front of them is just one or two seconds late after a traffic light turns green. Some people don't like to see a school bus because they know they might have to sit still for a few moments while children casually leave the bus.

When I first moved to Florida, I lived near a drawbridge that crossed the Intercoastal Waterway. On many occasions I sat in a long line of automobiles waiting for a single sailboat to leisurely pass through the drawbridge. I learned to accept this delay as part of life in this oceanside community. I allowed time for this possibility whenever I left for an appointment or meeting. Instead of becoming impatient, I learned to relax and worship the Lord while I enjoyed the beautiful scenery.

Some people react quite strongly when they have to wait in line at these bridges. I read a newspaper article where a reporter interviewed several drawbridge operators. These people told amazing stories about the verbal abuse they received. Some drivers cursed them. Sometimes people threw things at them.

I believe you have seen similar examples of impatience with drivers in the area where you live. Actuaries for automobile insurance companies have put a dollar value on our driving habits. Increasing automobile insurance rates reflect the impatience of many drivers.

Our generation also has exhibited increasing impatience in our eating habits. Jesus spoke of this impatience during His earthly ministry. He said, "...many were [continually] coming and going, and *they had not even leisure enough to eat*" (Mark 6:31).

Sometimes we're so busy that we skip meals or eat rapidly. In recent years this tendency has increased. The desire to eat quickly has caused thousands of fast food restaurants to spring up. More and more people gulp down their food and hurry to wherever they're going next. Many fast food restaurants have "drive through" windows so customers don't have to get out of their automobiles. Some of these restaurants guarantee a free meal if the food isn't ready within a specific time limit.

Many of us eat rapidly in our homes. The microwave oven has become a virtual necessity for some people. Our supermarkets are filled with a wide variety of foods that can be prepared quickly. Some people drink "instant" coffee and tea. When we finish eating, many of us put our dishes into an automatic dishwasher instead of washing them by hand.

I'm *not* saying everything I mention in this chapter is bad. Some of the conveniences I have mentioned and many of the conveniences I'm about to mention are an important part of my life. I'm thankful for them. However, I want to point out that all of these things can contribute to impatience.

We live in a "throw away" society. We discard many of the containers our food and drinks come in. Mothers everywhere appreciate disposable diapers. Sometimes we use paper napkins, paper cups, paper plates and plastic utensils so we can discard them when we're finished.

Many people have "instant" cameras so they can see pictures a few seconds after they're taken. Most film developers offer one day photo development so people with conventional cameras can receive their pictures as soon as possible. Some dry cleaning establishments offer one hour dry cleaning. Firms that offer rapid oil change and lubrication for automobiles have grown significantly during recent years.

People who want money from their bank accounts can receive instant cash from a money machine seven days a week at any hour of the day or night. The overnight mail industry has grown by leaps and bounds. Fax machines that transmit written messages instantly over the telephone have become have become almost essential to many of us. Millions of people use electronic mail to transmit messages on computers. Some people consistently talk on cellular telephones when they drive an automobile.

Many people fly regularly in jet airplanes. Travel agencies search their computers to find the fastest possible flight time from one place to another. Governmental agencies carefully monitor the arrival and departure rates of different airlines. These airlines are ranked by "on time performance" in ratings published in newspapers.

One night I was returning from a seminar in the midwest that required me to change planes in Chicago. My plane was delayed so I sat in O'Hare Airport at 11:00

p.m. on a Sunday night waiting for a connecting flight. While I waited, I was surprised by the large number of people who were hurriedly walking through the airport. Where did these people come from? Where were they going? Why were so many people in such a rush at a late hour on a Sunday night?

We often see impatience in supermarkets and other places where we have to wait in line. When we prepare to check out, many of us carefully examine the different lines at checkout booths in an attempt to find the shortest line. While writing this book, I was especially conscious of the many people who complained whenever a delay took place as they waited in a line.

Golf is one of my favorite hobbies. I have played golf for fifty years. Almost every time I play golf, I see people standing in a disgusted manner with their hands on their hips because they're so impatient with the slow pace of the people ahead of them. I have done this myself on several occasions. Slow play on golf courses has caused some people to forfeit enjoyment of the game.

We see signs of impatience from people who don't finish what they start. High school dropouts are a common problem today. Students become impatient with the demands of school. They leave because they want a more exciting lifestyle. Most professional sports now sign college athletes before they graduate.

We see more job hopping than ever before. In fact, changing employment has become part of many people's vocational planning. When these people start a new job, they don't expect to be there very long. It wasn't uncommon for our grandparents to work for the same employer from the time they finished high school until they retired. This custom is almost unheard of today.

We see a similar pattern with Christians jumping from church to church. When I first moved to Florida, I went to several different churches as I prayerfully sought the church I believed the Lord wanted me to join. When I found this church, I joined with every expectation of spending the rest of my life there. I'm *not* saying Christians shouldn't change churches. However, I often wonder if it is the Lord's will for so many Christians to jump from church to church.

We see another example of impatience by the accelerated interest in "get rich quick" schemes. We can see this impatience in the rapid growth of lotteries in recent years. Many state governments have profited because of the impatience of people who want to get rich in a hurry. I'm often surprised when I'm in a store to see the person in front of me pay a large amount of money for lottery tickets.

I don't believe lotteries are part of God's plan for our lives. The Word of God teaches that "get rich quick" schemes inevitably lead to problems. "He who has an evil and covetous eye hastens to be rich and knows not that want will come upon him" (Proverbs 28:22).

I have been a self-employed businessman for almost thirty years. By God's grace, my Christian business partner and I have enjoyed success in our business enterprises. I believe one reason the Lord has blessed us is because we are willing to do things the hard way. We never attempt to force immediate results. We take the narrow road instead of the wide road. We have learned to build our businesses on a long term value system instead of trying to force immediate results because we want to earn money rapidly.

We work each day to help others, not just to earn money. Greedy people inevitably look for quick ways to make money. Our Father doesn't want His children looking for short cuts. If we do, we go against God's instructions. "...the one greedy for gain curses and spurns, yes, renounces and despises the Lord" (Psalm 10:3).

Shortcuts usually lead to trouble. This is true in business and it is true in every other area of life. The seemingly easy way inevitably turns out to be the hardest way. Most people over the age of forty can attest to this truth based upon personal experience and from observing this trait in other people.

Another example of impatience can be seen in the restless lifestyle of many people who find it difficult to sit still. These people have to be doing something constantly. If they find themselves alone, they often pick up the telephone just to talk with someone. These people often turn on a radio, a cassette tape player or a CD player because they can't stand silence.

Some people find temporary relief for their impatience by turning on their television sets. Many of us have remote control devices that enable us to move continually from one channel to another. Some people change channels constantly as they look for something new and different to stimulate and excite them.

Videotape recorders have become a virtual necessity for many people. They don't want to miss anything. Some people record television programs so they can watch them later. Other people watch one program while they record a program on another channel at the same time.

I have followed sports for many years. I often think about the increasing impatience of sports fans. Many of these people are unhappy unless their team ranks #1. When two baseball teams go to the World Series and one team loses, many fans of the losing team are very unhappy. The winner of football's Super Bowl receives a lot of glory.

Sometimes the losers are treated as failures even though they have had an extremely successful season.

Most professional athletes know their fame is short-lived. They understand that many sports fans say, "What have you done for me lately?" Many sports fans are only satisfied if their teams win. Second place isn't good enough. Sometimes successful coaches are fired within a year or two after winning a major championship. Some great coaches have been criticized because they haven't produced championship teams for a year or two.

Another area where we see increasing impatience is in our relationships with members of our families. Parents often are frustrated with their children. Children are impatient with their parents. Divorce which was almost unheard of fifty years ago has become a common occurrence.

There has been a tremendous increase in installment buying in recent years. People aren't willing to wait. Because of this, our economy revolves around debt. We have become a credit card society. The interest payments on personal debts are staggering. Because of their impatience, many people have become financial slaves to credit card companies and lending institutions.

We have seen a similar pattern in our federal government. Our national debt has escalated rapidly in recent years. This debt now has reached a point that would have been incomprehensible to most people just a few years ago. Some state and local governments experience similar problems.

The faster we go, the faster we seem to want to go. Nothing seems to satisfy us. When we get one thing, we want something else. Many people don't understand that they receive their thrills from anticipation rather than realization. As soon as they get what they want, they become bored and want something else.

Some people describe their lives as a "rat race." They go at a feverish pace from early in the morning until late at night. Once again, I want to emphasize that everything I'm saying in this chapter *isn't* necessarily bad. However, there is no doubt that our generation lives at a much faster pace than any preceding generation.

In the first chapter, we studied God's Word to see the importance of patience. In the second chapter, we have looked at our current lifestyle to see why many people are impatient. In the next chapter, we'll look into the Word of God to study the patience of many well known people in the Bible.

Chapter 3

Biblical Examples of Patience and Perseverance

We'll start this chapter by looking into the Word of God to learn about the patience of Almighty God. Our Father is extremely patient as He looks down at a world filled with pride, selfishness and immorality. *No human being can begin to comprehend the patience of God* as He looks at abortion, sexual abuse, AIDS and other transgressions in the world today.

How can God continue to wait instead of sending Jesus back to earth immediately? The Word of God gives us the answer. "...He is *long-suffering, (extraordinarily patient)* toward you, *not* desiring that *any* should perish, but that *all* should turn to repentance" (II Peter 3:9).

There is a definite move of Satan in the world today. At the same time we see so much sin, we also see a great move of the Holy Spirit. "...where sin increased and abounded, *grace (God's unmerited favor) has surpassed it and increased the more and superabounded*" (Romans 5:20).

Our Father is gracious. He hates sin, but he loves sinners. He is very patient with everyone on earth. He doesn't want anyone to perish. Our Father wants every person on earth to have the opportunity to live eternally with Him in heaven.

In addition to being patient with the sins of unsaved people, our Father is patient with His children. He sees that some of us don't spend much time studying the Bible. Some Christians have an inadequate prayer life. Some of us don't praise Him very often, if at all. Unfortunately, many Christians fail to tell other people about eternal salvation through Jesus Christ. Some of us fail to give freely of the time, money and ability our Father has provided for us. Some of us are critical and unloving toward others.

In spite of these shortcomings, *our Father is very patient with each of His children.* He dislikes our sins, but He continues to love us in spite of our transgressions. "The Lord is gracious and full of compassion, slow to anger and abounding in mercy and loving-kindness" (Psalm 145:8).

We can see many examples of patience and perseverance in the life of Jesus Christ during His earthly ministry. The first recorded incident of His extraordinary patience occurred when Jesus was only twelve years old. At that time Jesus accompanied His parents to Jerusalem for the Passover Festival.

While the family was in Jerusalem, Jesus became separated from His parents. Joseph and Mary searched diligently for Jesus for three days. They finally found Him in the temple where the rabbis and others in attendance were amazed by the spiritual maturity of a twelve year old child. "And *all* who heard Him were *astonished* and *overwhelmed* with bewildered wonder at His intelligence and understanding and His replies" (Luke 2:47).

Joseph and Mary were distressed because their young son had been missing for three days. Jesus replied to their concern with a very interesting statement. "...He said to them, How is it that you had to look for Me? Did you not see and know that it is necessary [as a duty] for Me to be in *My Father's house* and [occupied] about *My Father's business?* But they did not comprehend what He was saying to them" (Luke 2:49-50).

These words give us a definite indication of the patience of Jesus Christ. At the young age of twelve, *Jesus knew He was the Son of God.* In spite of this knowledge, Jesus patiently lived in subjection to His earthly parents for many years. "And He went down with them and came to Nazareth *and was [habitually] obedient to them...*" (Luke 2:51).

Jesus didn't start His earthly ministry until He was thirty years old. He lived for at least *eighteen years* as a carpenter's son. He probably worked as a carpenter Himself even though He was extremely intelligent and knew throughout these years that He was the Son of God. Jesus understood why He had been sent to earth. He knew what was ahead of Him. He still waited very patiently.

Why did our Father make Jesus wait so long? We don't know the answer to this question. God obviously had a reason for this delay because His timing is always perfect. Perhaps one reason was to teach us about the extraordinary patience of God. Also, our Father wanted us to see this wonderful example of the patience of His Son.

At the age of thirty, Jesus began His earthly ministry. He started by choosing His apostles. Most of these men were rough, untrained working men. For three years, Jesus taught them great spiritual truths. Their response to His teaching often indicated that they didn't understand what He was telling them. In addition to learning very slowly, some of the apostles were proud and selfish. Jesus always was extremely patient with these men.

We see another example of the patience of Jesus in His relationship with Saul of Tarsus. Saul spent many years persecuting Christians. He committed several horrible atrocities. "...Saul shamefully treated and laid waste the church continuously [with cruelty and violence]; and entering house after house, he dragged out men and women and committed them to prison" (Acts 8:3).

Saul was an enemy of Jesus Christ. He did everything he could to destroy Jesus. One day a miracle happened to Saul. "...as he traveled on, he came near to Damascus, and suddenly a light from heaven flashed around him, and he fell to the ground. Then he heard a voice saying to him, Saul, Saul, *why* are you persecuting Me [harassing, troubling, and molesting Me]? And Saul said, Who are You, Lord? And He said, I am Jesus, Whom you are persecuting..." (Acts 9:3-5).

Jesus then instructed Saul to get up and go the city of Damascus. Saul was blind for three days. Other men had to lead him to Damascus. When they arrived, a man named Ananias was instructed by Jesus to pray for Saul. Ananias questioned these instructions. "...Ananias answered, Lord, I have heard many people tell about this man, especially how much evil and what great suffering he has brought on Your saints at Jerusalem..." (Acts 9:13).

Jesus patiently instructed Ananias to proceed. "So Ananias left and went into the house. And he laid his hands on Saul and said, Brother Saul, the Lord Jesus, Who appeared to you along the way by which you came here, has sent me that you may recover your sight and be filled with the Holy Spirit. And instantly something like scales fell from [Saul's] eyes, and he recovered his sight. Then he arose and was baptized" (Acts 9:17-18).

After this miracle, Saul's name was changed to Paul. He became the revered apostle Paul who traveled throughout the land proclaiming Christ. *Because of the patience of Jesus Christ,* Saul became a great Christian leader whose life has been an inspiration to millions of people.

Paul wrote several books in the New Testament. In a letter to Timothy, Paul said, "...I obtained mercy for the reason that in me, as *the foremost [of sinners], Jesus Christ might show forth and display all His perfect long-suffering and patience* for an *example* to [encourage] those who would thereafter believe on Him for [the gaining of] eternal life" (I Timothy 1:16).

Paul referred to his life as Saul by calling himself *the foremost of sinners*. He said that Jesus exhibited perfect patience as an *example* to encourage people that He really is the Messiah Who can provide eternal life in heaven. Many millions of people have been blessed because Jesus was extraordinarily patient with Saul of Tarsus.

We see another amazing example of patience during the final hours before Jesus was crucified. After Jesus and His apostles finished the Last Supper, they climbed the Mount of Olives to a garden on the side of the mountain. This garden was called the Garden of Gethesemane.

Jesus was fully aware of the terrible ordeal that awaited Him. He wondered if there was any way He could escape this agony. "And going a little farther, He fell on the ground and kept praying that *if* it were possible the [fatal] hour might *pass from Him*. And He was saying, Abba, [which means] Father, everything is possible for You. *Take away* this cup from Me: yet *not what I will, but what You [will]*" (Mark 14:35-36).

Jesus didn't want to pay the tremendous price He had to pay. In His humanness He asked God if He could be spared from what was ahead of Him. Yet, in the next breath, Jesus said that He wanted to do God's will not His own.

After Jesus was arrested, He went through a mockery of "trials" before several different Jewish and Roman officials. Jesus exhibited *great patience* throughout each of these trials. He maintained His composure even though He was treated unfairly.

Jesus then was beaten horribly, marched through the streets of Jerusalem and crucified at Calvary. People taunted Him and made fun of Him while He suffered. Nevertheless, Jesus was patient, compassionate and forgiving throughout this horrible ordeal. As He hung on the cross, *"...Jesus prayed, Father, forgive them for they know not what they do..."* (Luke 23:34).

When we go through adversity in our lives, *Jesus wants us to be patient as He was patient.* *"...He, for the joy [of obtaining the prize] that was set before Him, endured the cross, despising and ignoring the shame, and is now seated at the right hand of the throne of God. Just think of Him Who endured from sinners such grievous opposition and bitter hostility against Himself [reckon up and consider it all in comparison with your trials], so that you may not grow weary or exhausted, losing heart and relaxing and fainting in your minds"* (Hebrews 12:2-3).

Jesus despised the shame of what He went through, but He ignored it. He accepted what He had to endure. Jesus was able to do this because He focused His entire attention on the joy of the prize that was set before Him. He knew the price He paid would set hundreds of millions of people free. *Jesus was able to see beyond the pain of the ordeal He was going through.* He focused on the magnificent reward many people would receive as a result of His sacrifice.

No one has ever had to put up with anything like the tremendous anguish Jesus endured. This passage of Scripture instructs us to *compare our trials with what He went through.* If we follow these instructions, *the example of Jesus will help us to endure adversity. We won't become weary and give up.*

Some people might think Jesus was able to do these things because He is God. *Jesus went through this suffering as a human being just like we are.* *"...because He Himself [in His humanity] has suffered in being tempted (tested and tried), He is able [immediately] to run to the cry of (assist, relieve) those who are being tempted and tested and tried [and who therefore are being exposed to suffering]"* (Hebrews 2:18).

Whenever we go through a season of adversity, we should realize that Jesus has endured everything we will go through and much, much more. Because Jesus suffered in His humanity, He is able to strengthen us in our trials. Jesus wants us to focus on Him so we can keep going in His strength.

The word "Christian" means "Christ-like." Jesus wants us to be steady, consistent and dependable as He is. Jesus lives in our hearts. *His patience is available to us.* He wants us to be patient because we have been given *"...the steadfastness and patience [of Christ]"* (Titus 2:2).

We see another interesting example of patience in the story of Noah building the ark. When Noah started, this project must have seemed incongruous to people who watched what he was doing. *No one on earth had seen rain.* *"...the Lord God had not [yet] caused it to rain upon the earth..."* (Genesis 2:5).

There were no rivers, lakes or streams on the earth at that time. God provided the water the earth needed through mist that rose from the ground. Apparently, the people went out each morning to gather up enough moisture from dew to last throughout the day. *"...there went up a mist (fog, vapor) from the land and watered the whole surface of the ground..."* (Genesis 2:6).

Noah lived in this environment when God looked at the wickedness of the world and told Noah to build an ark. "God said to Noah, I intend to make an end of all flesh, for through men the land is filled with violence; and behold, I will destroy them and the land. Make yourself an ark of gopher or cypress wood; make in it rooms (stalls, pens, coops, nests, cages, and compartments) and cover it inside and out with pitch (bitumen)" (Genesis 6:13-14).

God gave Noah specific instructions for the ark. "And this is the way you are to make it: the length of the ark shall be 300 cubits, its breadth 50 cubits, and its height 30 cubits, [that is, 450 ft. x 75 ft. x 45 ft.]. You shall make a roof or window [a place for light] for the ark and finish it to a cubit [at least 18 inches] above — and the door of the ark you shall put in the side of it; and you shall make it with lower, second, and third stories" (Genesis 6:15-16).

Even though Noah had never seen water except for mists, he patiently carried out these specific instructions. Noah spent approximately *one hundred years* building this ark. Genesis 5:32 says that Noah was five hundred years old just before God told him to build the ark. Genesis 7:6 says he was six hundred years old when the earth was flooded.

How much patience did Noah have to have during the one hundred years he spent building the ark? People must have ridiculed him, but he continued to build this huge boat. When they asked Noah why he was doing this, he could only reply that a great flood was coming upon the earth.

In addition to building the ark, God gave Noah another assignment that required tremendous patience. "And of every living thing of all flesh [found on land], you shall bring two of every sort into the ark, to keep them alive with you; they shall be male and female. Of fowls and birds according to their kinds, of beasts according to their kinds, of every creeping thing of the ground according to its kind — two of every sort shall come in with you, that they may be kept alive. Also take with you every sort of food that is eaten, and you shall collect and store it up, and it shall serve as food for you and for them" (Genesis 6:19-21).

Imagine how difficult it must have been for one man to build this huge ark. Then, Noah had to locate one male and one female *of every species of living thing.* This assignment was very difficult to carry out. We can't begin to comprehend the thousands of different varieties of birds and animals that Noah had to locate *and trap alive.* He couldn't kill any of them. Noah had to capture one male and one female of each species. This project must have taken many years to complete.

In addition, Noah also was instructed to locate, transport and store tons of different kinds of food for these birds and animals to eat while they were in the ark. The logistics of this task are mind-boggling. *The job of building the ark, trapping the animals and supplying adequate food required immense patience over a long period of time.*

Job was another man who exhibited great patience. Job said, "...He knows the way that I take [He has concern for it, appreciates, and pays attention to it]. When He has tried me, I shall come forth as refined gold [pure and luminous]. *My foot has held fast to His steps; His ways have I kept and not turned aside. I have not gone back from the commandment of His lips; I have esteemed and treasured the words of His mouth more than my necessary food"* (Job 23:10-12).

This passage of Scripture explains why Job was able to be patient in the face of severe adversity. He knew God was concerned with what he was going through. He also realized that he would come out as "refined gold" if he didn't give up. Job was able to endure patiently because he refused to turn aside from the treasured instructions in the Word of God. Job knew his spiritual food was much more important than the food that fueled his body.

Job and many other prophets were required to have great patience. God blessed them for their patience. *"[As] an example of suffering and ill-treatment together with patience, brethren, take the prophets who spoke in the name of the Lord [as His messengers]. You know how we call those blessed (happy) who were steadfast [who endured]. You have heard of the endurance of Job, and you have seen the Lord's [purpose and how He richly blessed him in the] end, inasmuch as the Lord is full of pity and compassion and tenderness and mercy"* (James 5:10-11).

Job was extremely patient. He endured many severe trials and tribulations. *As a result of Job's patient endurance, the Lord blessed him greatly in his latter days. This reward for Job's patience should inspire us to be patient.*

Anyone who has carefully read the Psalms realizes that the Psalmist David often waited patiently for the Lord. At one point, David cried out to the Lord saying, *"How long will You forget me, O Lord? Forever? How long will You hide Your face from me? How long must I lay up cares within me and have sorrow in my heart day after day? How long shall my enemy exalt himself over me? Consider and answer me, O Lord my God; lighten the eyes [of my faith to behold Your face in the pitchlike darkness], lest I sleep the sleep of death"* (Psalm 13:1-3).

David asked the Lord "how long?" four times in this one passage of Scripture. Some of us have been in similar situations. We have waited and waited for God to bless us. Sometimes it seems as if He has completely forgotten us. *God never forgets us.* We should be encouraged because God heard David's cry and answered it.

God didn't answer immediately, *but He did answer*. "I waited *patiently* and *expectantly* for the Lord; and *He inclined to me and heard my cry*. He drew me up out of a horrible pit [a pit of tumult and of destruction], out of the miry clay (froth and slime), and set my feet upon a rock, steadying my steps and establishing my goings. And He has put a new song in my mouth, a song of praise to our God. Many shall see and fear (revere and worship) and put their trust and confident reliance in the Lord" (Psalm 40:1-3).

God lifted David out of darkness and put him in a wonderful new environment. David was exhilarated. He sang songs of praise and thanksgiving. He knew his experience would help many people to build their trust in the Lord and to wait patiently for Him.

Each of these examples from the Bible should be a source of encouragement to us today. I'd like to briefly mention one final person who was a wonderful example to all of us — the beloved apostle Paul. *He endured patiently on many occasions because he knew he could trust God*. "...I *know* (perceive, have knowledge of, and am acquainted with) Him Whom I have believed (adhered to and trusted in and relied on), and *I am [positively] persuaded* that He is able to guard and keep that which has been entrusted to me and which I have committed [to Him]..." (II Timothy 1:12).

Paul was persecuted again and again. He traveled many miles under excruciating conditions. He was shipwrecked, bitten by a poisonous snake, stoned, arrested and imprisoned. Paul never gave up. He praised the Lord continually. I'll use other examples pertaining to Paul in later chapters, but I wanted to briefly include him here as well.

I ask each person reading this book, *what situation are you faced with in your life that requires patience?* Do you need to be more patient with your spouse, your children, your parents or your in-laws? Do you need to be more patient with your neighbors, your employer or people who work with you? Do you need to be patient with a difficult or frustrating situation?

Compare your need for patience with the patience required by God, Jesus, Noah, Job, David and Paul. Meditate on the Scripture references in this chapter. Realize that the same Holy Spirit who enabled these men to be incredibly patient lives inside of you. *Ask Him to give you the patience you need one day at a time. Believe He will answer your prayer.*

I hope these examples from the Bible will help you to be more patient. In the next chapter, we'll study God's Word to learn all we can about another subject that will help you to be more patient. We'll learn many facts about God's timing and why our Father's timing is very different from our timing.

Chapter 4

God's Perfect Timing

Most of us look at life from the perspective of the seventy, eighty or ninety years we expect to live on earth. Most of our goals and aspirations are based upon this period of time. We say, "When the children finish college" ... "When the mortgage is paid off" ... "When we retire" and similar things.

I don't believe it's wrong to think this way. God looks at us from this time frame, but He also evaluates our lives from an *eternal perspective*. God's timing is quite different from ours. *"...do not let this one thought escape you, beloved, that with the Lord one day is as a thousand years and a thousand years as one day. The Lord does not delay and is not tardy or slow about what He promises, according to some people's conception of slowness..."* (II Peter 3:8-9).

If we want to be more patient we should attempt to look at the events in our lives from God's eternal perspective instead of a carnal, earthly perspective. Many middle-aged and older people can look back on their lives and see the lessons they have learned and the growth they experienced when severe problems in their lives forced them to become more patient.

Our Father is never late. He may seem to be slow, but He isn't. His timing doesn't conform to earthly timing.

We must understand how short a period of one thousand years is from His perspective. "For a thousand years in Your sight are but *as yesterday* when it is past, or as a *watch in the night*" (Psalm 90:4).

To God, one thousand years is like yesterday was to you and me. From His eternal perspective, one thousand years is like a few hours that someone spent when this was written working as a watchman during the night.

We must realize that our Father's timing is more precise than the most sophisticated timing device ever invented on earth. He has ordained *an exact and specific time for everything.* "To *everything* there is a season, and a time for *every* matter or purpose under heaven..." (Ecclesiastes 3:1).

We're all familiar with the seasons of spring, summer, fall and winter. Each of these seasons has a beginning and an end. I am often comforted when I'm going through a difficult period of time in my life by saying, "The Bible says *everything* is for a *season. There is an end* to this ordeal I'm facing. I trust You, Father, to bring me safely through this season in my life. Thank you, dear Father."

Sometimes we deeply desire to receive an answer from God and we wonder why He hasn't answered our prayers. *We must learn to trust God's timing just as we trust Him in every other area.* The prophet Habakkuk was given a vision by the Lord. The Lord told Habakkuk this vision would be manifested at a specific time. He said, "...the vision is yet for *an appointed time* and it hastens to the end [fulfillment]; *it will not deceive or disappoint.* Though it tarry, *wait [earnestly] for it,* because *it will surely come*; it will *not* be behindhand on its appointed day" (Habakkuk 2:3).

Has God given you a clear vision of what He wants you to do with your life? Are you impatient because nothing seems to be happening? I know what it is to be in the center of God's will and, at the same time, to be frustrated with the apparent lack of progress.

Eighteen years ago God gave me a clear vision of the ministry He had for me. I have been faithful to this ministry ever since that time. In all honesty, many of the things God showed me haven't taken place. I'm still learning to be patient while I continue to wait for God's *appointed time which will surely come.*

This principle that the Lord explained to Habakkuk applies to every child of God. Our Father's timing is perfect. If we question His timing, we sin. *We should give up all anxiety about the timing of God and let Him answer when He chooses to answer. "My times are in Your hands..."* (Psalm 31:15).

Our Father doesn't want us to be impatient with Him. Instead, He wants us to say something like the following. "My times are in Your hands, Father. I'll do my best to live my life the way I believe you want me to live it. Then, I'll trust You to bring the answers to my prayers in Your way and in Your good timing."

Our Father doesn't want us to be impatient. If we continually seek His will and do our best to live in accordance with the instructions in His Word, we have every right to believe He will answer our prayers in the proper time. *"And let us not lose heart and grow weary and faint in acting nobly and doing right, for in due time and at the appointed season we shall reap, if we do not loosen and relax our courage and faint"* (Galatians 6:9).

This promise is *conditional.* Please note the word *if.* We *will* reap a harvest in due time from the seeds we have sown *if* we do not loosen and relax our courage and faint. We *can* fail to reap the harvest our Father wants to give us. If we want to receive this harvest, we *must not give up no matter how long we have to wait.*

Some of us block our Father from giving us the manifestation of the answer to our prayers because we aren't willing to wait long enough. Please notice the words I have put in italics in the last two paragraphs. Focus on these words. Be willing to wait for God's answer to your prayers in His *appointed season.*

We shouldn't miss out on receiving the answer to God's conditional promises. Often these promises are made based upon the condition of our faith and our patience. Our Father knows exactly what He's doing. We must have faith in Him and we must wait patiently for Him.

Our Father is the Master Planner. Sometimes we ask Him for an immediate answer without realizing there are several pieces He still must fit into place. We may be ready to receive God's answer to our prayers, but we often have to wait until God fits other pieces together. Our deadline and God's deadline often are different. *We don't set deadlines. God sets deadlines.*

Sometimes it seems as if a season of adversity will never end. From God's perspective, we often don't suffer as long as we think. "...after you have suffered *a little while*, the God of all grace [Who imparts all blessing and favor], Who has called you to His [own] eternal glory in Christ Jesus, *will Himself complete and make you what you ought to be*, establish and ground you securely, and strengthen, and settle you" (I Peter 5:10).

This passage of Scripture speaks of suffering for *a little while*. When we have to wait for God's answer, I think we should say something like the following. "Dear Father, I believe You want me to learn something from this season of adversity. Please show me what You want me to learn.

In Jesus' name, I ask You to help me become what You want me to become."

When we go through a season of adversity, we shouldn't grumble and complain. Instead, we should realize that God has a purpose for what is happening to us. *If we wait faithfully and patiently, He will complete us and make us what we ought to be. He will strengthen us and build us up.*

Many times we can wait much longer than we think we can. The Bible is filled with thousands of promises. Our Father tells us again and again what He will do, *but He never tells us when we will receive these promises.* *"...my words are of a kind which will be fulfilled in the appointed and proper time"* (Luke 1:20).

Some of us make the mistake of trying to get God to conform to our plans and our timing instead of continually seeking His plan for our lives and trusting in His timing. Our Father knows what He wants to do in each of our lives and He knows when He wants to do it.

For example, God knew exactly when He wanted Jesus to start His earthly ministry. From a human point of view, we might wonder why God didn't send Jesus to earth long before He did. However, our Father knew exactly when the time was right for Jesus to be born of the virgin Mary. "...when the *proper time* had fully come, God sent His Son, born of a woman..." (Galatians 4:4).

Jesus understood His Father's perfect timing. He never rushed. Once, when His brothers urged Him to go to Judea, "...Jesus said to them, My time (opportunity) has *not* come yet..." (John 7:6). Jesus refused to go before His Father's time. "...my time is *not* ripe. [My term is *not* yet completed; it is *not* time for Me to go]" (John 7:8).

Shortly after Jesus said this, Jewish leaders were unable to arrest Him even though they wanted to do so. God's plan for our lives is based upon His intricate timing. "...they were eager to arrest Him, but no one laid a hand on Him, for His hour (time) had *not* yet come" (John 7:30).

Jesus was filled with the Holy Spirit and controlled by the Holy Spirit throughout His earthly ministry. Jesus never raced ahead of the Holy Spirit. He always lived in the Holy Spirit's perfect timing.

Jesus understood His Father's timing. He knew exactly when the time had come for Him to die on the cross, to be resurrected from the dead and to return to His Father. "...before the Passover Feast began, Jesus knew (was fully aware) that *the time had come* for Him to leave this world and return to the Father..." (John 13:1).

These passages of Scripture provide insight into God's precise timing. We can't understand God's timing with our limited human comprehension. *"...It is not for you to become acquainted with and know what time brings* [the things and events of time and their definite periods] or fixed years and seasons (their critical niche in time), which the Father has appointed (fixed and reserved) by His own choice and authority and personal power" (Acts 1:7).

The future belongs to God. Our Father wants us to live in the present, trusting Him one day at a time. Many of the aspects pertaining to our Father's timing are beyond human comprehension. Unfortunately, some of us rise too often to occasions that don't need to be risen to. As I grow older, I'm finally starting to learn to relax and trust my Father's timing.

God's delay is not necessarily a denial. Sometimes we think our Father is denying us when He just wants us to wait a little longer. *Should we trust God in every other area of our lives and not trust His timing?* Unfortunately, this is exactly what some Christians do.

Our Father is completely dependable. He *will* do what His Word says He will do, but sometimes the waiting period for His answer can be weeks, months or years. Our Father knows when He wants to bless us. When He spoke to His people through the prophet Haggai, He told them "...From *this day on* I will bless you" (Haggai 2:19). Our Father knew He wanted to release His blessings to His people at that time. He also knows when He wants to bless us today.

Our impatience is an insult to God. Although most of us don't actually say the following words, our impatience actually says, "God, You don't know when to give me an answer to my prayers. I need this answer now. Don't wait any longer. Give me what I want and give it to me now!"

If you're tempted to rush God, please review the fifteen Scripture references in this chapter. Put them in the first person. Personalize them. Meditate upon them. Try to understand timing from God's point of view. You'll be much happier if you do.

Chapter 5

God Doesn't Want Us to Hurry

We have looked carefully at the impatient, fast paced lifestyle in the world today. We have compared this with the patience of God, Jesus, Noah, Job, the psalmist David and the apostle Paul. We have studied God's Word to learn many facts about our Father's perfect timing. God doesn't want us to hurry.

Our Father never hurries. He is always at peace. We see a divine order in everything He does. There is *no* place in His Word where we are instructed to hurry. Instead, we should be calm and still while we wait patiently. *"Be still and rest in the Lord; wait for Him and patiently lean yourself upon Him..."* (Psalm 37:7).

When we pray and nothing seems to be happening some of us have a tendency to try to rush things. Instead, our Father wants us to be still. We should rest in Him and wait patiently for His answer. We should lean on God because we trust Him completely.

Our Father has a perfect rhythm. Each day He causes ocean tides to come in and go out on a definite, precise schedule. The sun rises at a predictable time each morning. It sets at a specific time each night. The moon changes four times each month at a predetermined time. "[The Lord] appointed the moon for the seasons; the sun knows [the exact time] of its setting" (Psalm 104:19).

If you live near the ocean, your local newspaper will publish the exact times each day when the tides come in and go out. We all can read the exact time of sunrise and sunset. We are told exactly when each season of the moon will begin and end. How can the people who provide this information to a newspaper, a radio station or a television station know these times so accurately? They can predict these times to the minute because God is perfect and *He sets these times.*

Our Father wants us to tune in to His perfect rhythm and timing. *We must not get ahead of Him.* I know how it is to do things too rapidly. I tend to be high strung and intense. The roots of these characteristics go back to my childhood. I'm always on the go. I constantly have to fight the urge to rush. I often meditate on specific Scripture references to help me slow down.

On the other hand, my wife is always calm and collected. She never races ahead of the Lord. She doesn't try to force things to happen. Opposites attract because she and I are different in many ways. Sometimes I wish I could be more like she is. I have improved in this area, but I have to work at this continually.

High strung, negative, intense, self-centered people tend to rush. Calm, composed, God-centered people are better able to discern the Lord's timing and trust in Him. Can you imagine Jesus being out of control and rushing ahead of His Father? Jesus never hurried during His earthly ministry. As we study the four gospels, we see that Jesus consistently remained calm when He was under severe pressure.

We see an example of this calmness by His reaction when Lazarus, the brother of Mary and Martha, became very sick. Jesus had just healed many people. He was very close to Mary and Martha. It would seem reasonable that

49

He would want to heal Lazarus. When Jesus heard about this sickness, did He drop everything to immediately rush to the side of Lazarus? "...[even] when He heard that Lazarus was sick, *He still stayed two days longer* in the same place where He was" (John 11:6).

When Jesus finally went to Bethany where Lazarus was, it *seemed* as if He was too late. *Did Jesus miss God's timing when He arrived to find that Lazarus had died before He came?* "...when Jesus arrived, He found that he [Lazarus] *had already been in the tomb four days*" (John 11:17).

When Martha heard Jesus was coming, she went out to meet Him. Martha knew her brother would still be alive if Jesus had arrived in time. "Martha then said to Jesus, Master, if *You had been here, my brother would not have died*" (John 11:21).

Instead of berating Jesus and complaining about the delay, Martha did just the opposite. *She told Jesus she knew He still was not too late.* Martha said, *"And even now I know that whatever You ask from God, He will grant it to You"* (John 11:22).

Shortly after Martha expressed her faith, Jesus raised Lazarus from the dead. "...He shouted with a loud voice, Lazarus, come out! *And out walked the man who had been dead,* his hands and feet wrapped in burial cloths (linen strips), and with a [burial] napkin bound around his face. Jesus said to them, Free him of the burial wrappings and let him go" (John 11:43-44).

This story has been included in the Bible to teach us to be patient with God's timing. From a human point of view, Jesus should have rushed to heal Lazarus. From God's point of view, He wanted Jesus to wait so Martha could express her faith that Jesus could raise Lazarus from the dead.

Satan wants us to become discouraged if we don't receive an answer when we think we should. Satan is impatient. He often rushes and tries to make things happen. God wants us to be like He is. As we wrestle with difficult problems, will we identify with Satan's impatience or with God's perfect timing? Will we pick up the fast pace of the world we live in or will we be able to exhibit God's calmness and composure?

We must turn away from the ways of the world. Satan is referred to as "*...the god of this world...*" (II Corinthians 4:4). He orchestrates the fast pace of the world. "*...the whole world [around us] is under the power of the evil one*" (I John 5:19).

Christians should not be worldly in any way. If we are carnal in any area of our lives, we open the door to Satan in this area. We must not allow ourselves to get caught up with the fast pace of this world. Satan tries to push us. He wants us to rush, hurry and worry. We must not give in to his urging.

Jesus won a complete victory over Satan. Spiritual discipline and maturity are required to turn away from the pace of the world to quietly and patiently wait on the Lord. The best way to turn away from the world is to get quiet time alone with the Lord on a consistent basis. He is the hub around which our lives should revolve. Christians who consistently spend time alone with the Lord are able to identify with the perfect rhythm of the Holy Spirit. They won't be caught up in the hectic pace of the world.

I have been a self-employed businessman for almost thirty years. I understand the extreme pressure that business owners often face. If I'm in control of my life, I tend to hurry and worry. However, I'm still learning that Christians whose lives really are under the control of the Holy Spirit can remain calm in the midst of a hectic situation.

This calmness comes more naturally to some people than to others. If you tend to be hurried and tense like I am, I urge you to slow down each day. Study and meditate on the Word of God. Take time to pray and worship the Lord. Yield control of your life to the Holy Spirit. Ask Him to live His life in you and through you.

We must not race ahead of God. Too many of us worry about the future. Instead, we should patiently trust the Lord one day at a time. Jesus said, "...*do not worry or be anxious about tomorrow*, for tomorrow will have worries and anxieties of its own. Sufficient for *each day* is its own trouble" (Matthew 6:34).

Our Father wants each of His children to live in "day-tight compartments." He wants us to lock the door to yesterday. He wants us to lock the door to tomorrow. We must not dwell in the past or in the future. Our Father created us to live one day at a time.

Unfortunately, some of us tend to cross bridges before we come to them. If we make this mistake, we waste emotional energy. If we worry about the future, we dilute our effectiveness in the present. Jesus said, "Give us *daily* our bread [food for the morrow]" (Luke 11:3).

Jesus didn't ask His Father to provide food for a week, a month, a year or for several years. He asked His Father for food for one day. *Christians who learn to live one day at a time will be calm. They will have more patience, faith and spiritual strength.* "...as your *day*, so shall your strength, your rest and security, be" (Deuteronomy 33:25).

Our Father will give us the strength we need one day at a time. He wants us to rest in faith in our knowledge of His provision. He gives each of His children perfect security one day at a time.

Our Father doesn't want us to succumb to external pressure. As we grow and mature as Christians, the hectic pace of an externally oriented world will affect us less and less. We'll live our lives from the inside out, not from the outside in. We'll realize that our Father has provided everything we need within us. *"...the kingdom of God is within you [in your hearts]..."* (Luke 17:21).

The Holy Spirit lives in our hearts. He wants us to identify with Him continually. If we do this, we will remain still and calm. Whenever my life gets too hectic, I often meditate on the following passage of Scripture. *"...be still, and know (recognize and understand) that I am God..."* (Psalm 46:10).

I can't tell you how many times these words have quieted and calmed me when I was faced with severe problems. Whenever I meditate on these words and personalize them and think about what they really mean, I can hear my Father telling me to be still. A sense of calmness always comes over me as I meditate on the meaning of these words.

When I'm tempted to worry and hurry, I often open my mouth and say something like the following. "Dear Father, *I will be still.* I will quiet down and calm down because I *know* You are God. I'm certain You will take care of everything if I'll just remain calm and trust in You and wait on You."

We live in a world that seems to be in a continual state of disarray. In the midst of seeming turmoil, we must realize that our Father is in complete control. Sometimes if doesn't look as if God is in control, but our Father is Almighty God, not "Part Mighty" God. He is omnipotent. He has total authority over everything that takes place in the universe. *We must be still and know that He is God!*

If the Holy Spirit really is in control of our lives, we'll be able to remain calm under pressure because He is always calm. If we hurry and rush and try to make things happen, we block the Holy Spirit Who never hurries. We can only hear His still, small voice if we're calm and relaxed.

Hurry rushes ahead of the Holy Spirit. Hurry rhymes with worry. Hurry and worry go together. *Hurry is worry in action.* Hurry is an outward manifestation of inner tension. If we hurry and rush ahead of God, we sin by missing the goals He has for us. *"...to be overhasty is to sin and miss the mark"* (Proverbs 19:2).

When we're under pressure, we should allow the Holy Spirit to set the pace. If we insist on rushing ahead of Him, He will allow us to do this. He gives us freedom of choice. However, we're headed for problems when we rush ahead of the Holy Spirit. Haste makes waste. Hurry causes many accidents.

No one has to study the Word of God to learn how to hurry. Hurry comes naturally to us. We inherited this tendency from our ancestor, Adam. Many people are influenced to hurry by the urging of Satan and his evil spirits. We need to study God's Word to learn to trust our Father so we can remain calm under pressure. "...he who *believes* (trusts in, relies on, and adheres to that Stone) will *not* be ashamed or give way or hasten away [in sudden panic]" (Isaiah 28:16).

As we study God's Word, we can clearly see that we make a big mistake when we rush ahead of the Lord. If we do this, we definitely will experience problems. *Every* person who is impatient will find that continued impatience always causes problems. *"...everyone who is impatient and hasty hastens only to want"* (Proverbs 21:5).

We block God's power if we race ahead of Him. Speed always operates at the expense of power. We can see an example of this by observing the gear ratios of an automobile engine. The lower the gear, the more power the engine produces. If we move to higher gears, the engine produces more speed and less power.

Patience requires us to idle the motor when we feel like stripping the gears. Unfortunately, some of us "strip our gears" because we race ahead of the Lord. In our attempt to save time, we usually lose more than we gain.

The first five chapters of this book are filled with specific instructions from God's Word pertaining to the subject of patience. I'd like to close these chapters on patience with the one Scripture reference that has helped me more than any other to increase my patience. In his letter to the Galatians, the apostle Paul said, "...*the fruit of the [Holy] Spirit [the work which His presence within accomplishes]* is love, joy, (gladness), peace, *patience (an even temper, forbearance)...*" (Galatians 5:22).

Paul went on to list additional fruit of the Spirit, but the one we are concerned with here is patience. If we really want to increase our patience, we must yield control of our lives to the Holy Spirit Who is always patient. Whenever I find myself doing something impatient, I try to realize this impatience is a clear indication that I'm attempting to control my life instead of allowing the Holy Spirit to live His life in me and through me. There is a direct ratio between the patience we exhibit and the amount of control we allow the Holy Spirit to have in our lives.

Chapter 6

Walk in the Victory of Jesus Christ

There is fine line between patience and perseverance. In the first five chapters of this book, I have written primarily about the subject of patience. In the remaining chapters, we'll study the Word of God to see how to obtain the perseverance that is required to solve many problems.

Some of the problems in our lives are caused by Satan. Some are caused by our own actions. Others are caused by events that take place in our lives. It is very important to learn everything we can about perseverance so we can bring the victory of Jesus Christ into manifestation when we face problems..

The blood of Jesus has changed all Christians from losers into winners. His shed blood enabled us to escape the horrors of hell and to live eternally in the beauty of heaven. *Every* problem will be overcome there. "God will wipe away *every tear* from their eyes; and *death shall be no more,* neither shall there be *anguish* (*sorrow* and *mourning*) nor *grief* nor *pain* any more, for the old conditions and the former order of things have *passed away*" (Revelation 21:4).

We must understand that the same victory we will experience in heaven is available to us here on earth! This victory is automatic in heaven. Everyone there shares in the victory of Jesus Christ. His victory *isn't* automatic here on earth. We must walk in *faith*. We must *persevere*.

Jesus also paid the price for us to walk in His victory during our lives on earth. We must not give up! Jesus said, "...*All* authority (*all* power of rule) in heaven and on earth has been given to Me" (Matthew 28:18). Jesus didn't say He has some authority and power. *He has all authority and all power in heaven and on earth.* What problems do you face? Jesus won a victory over every problem. He is in complete control.

By faith, we must believe that the victorious Jesus Christ lives inside of us. He wants us to rely completely upon Him. "...*it is no longer I who live, but Christ (the Messiah) lives in me; and the life I now live in the body I live by faith in (by adherence to and reliance on and complete trust in) the Son of God, Who loved me and gave Himself up for me*" (Galatians 2:20).

Are you going through a difficult time? Believe that Jesus Christ lives in your heart. Trust completely in Him. Believe that Jesus has absolute power and authority over everything on earth. Give up your right to control your life. Let Jesus live His life in you and through you. His victory is your victory. Refuse to give up!

Every child of God has been given the opportunity to partake of the victory of Jesus Christ. "For *whatever* is born of God *is victorious over the world*; and this is the victory *that conquers the world, even our faith. Who* is it that is victorious over [that conquers] the world but he who *believes* that Jesus is the Son of God [who adheres to, trusts in, and relies on that fact]?" (I John 5:4-5).

This passage of Scripture doesn't refer to the victory we will experience in heaven. It says everyone who has been reborn spiritually *is victorious over the world.* We are told that the victory of Jesus *conquers the world.* How do we bring this victory into manifestation when we struggle with the problems of life here on earth? We walk in this victory *by faith.* We must believe that Jesus is the Son of God and trust completely in the victory He has won for us. "...thanks be to God, Who in Christ *always* leads us in triumph [as trophies of Christ's victory]..." (II Corinthians 2:14).

We should thank God because He *always* leads us in triumph because of the victory of Jesus Christ. Please highlight or underline the word *always* in this passage of Scripture. We don't triumph some of the time. *We always triumph!* We will always walk in the victory of Jesus Christ *if* we really believe and *if* we persevere and refuse to give up.

We should expect to experience severe problems during our lives on earth. Jesus said, "...In the world you have *tribulations* and *trials* and *distress* and *frustration...*" (John 16:33). Jesus didn't stop there. He went on to say, "...*but be of good cheer [take courage; be confident, certain, undaunted]! For I have overcome the world [I have deprived it of power to harm you and have conquered it for you]*" (John 16:33).

The preceding Scripture reference is a good example of why I really like *The Amplified Bible* for a study Bible. Instead of just saying "I have overcome the world," this passage of Scripture is amplified to tell us that *Jesus has deprived the world of power to harm us. Jesus has conquered the world for us.* We must believe this!

Are you faced with tribulations, trials, distress and frustration? Jesus told us we should *expect* to have these problems. However, we shouldn't do what many people do. We shouldn't emphasize the problem. Jesus said we

58

should be cheerful, courageous and confident because He won a victory over our problems.

We can trust completely in Jesus. He won't let us down. *If* our faith is strong and *if* we refuse to give up, *we won't be sorry.* The Scripture says *"No man* who *believes in Him [who adheres to, relies on, and trusts in Him] will [ever] be put to shame or be disappointed"* (Romans 10:11).

Please highlight or underline the words *no man.* This promise applies to *you.* However, this promise is conditional. God promises that no Christian will ever be put to shame or disappointed, but we have to do our part. We must have strong and persevering faith in Jesus Christ.

God's Word is filled with thousands of promises. Our Father stands behind *every one* of His promises. We can depend on them! "...Know in all your hearts and in all your souls that not one thing has failed of all the good things which the Lord your God promised concerning you. *All have come to pass for you; not one thing of them has failed"* (Joshua 23:14).

When we're faced with problems, we should study and meditate continually on the Word of God. *Our Father wants us to fill our minds and hearts with His promises.* We can bring these promises into manifestation through strong, persevering faith. Our Father honors strong faith that perseveres.

We must realize that all Christians are actually members of the royal family of God. Our Father is Almighty God. Our brother, Jesus Christ, is the "...*King of kings and Lord of lords"* (Revelation 19:6). Because of the victory Jesus won for us, we "...*reign as kings in life* through the one Man Jesus Christ (the Messiah, the Anointed One)" (Romans 5:17).

Do you *really believe* you reign as a king in your life here on earth? We all will reign in heaven, but this passage of Scripture says we reign as kings *in life.* The victory of Jesus Christ belongs to us *now.* We must believe this. We must persevere.

The manifestation of the victory of Jesus Christ requires more than "head knowledge" of the promises in God's Word. We must *know* what the Word of God says, *but we also must believe these promises in our hearts.* We learn the promises in the Word of God by studying the Bible. However, these promises can only get from our minds into our hearts when we meditate on them day and night.

Are you faced with difficult problems? Saturate yourself in the magnificent promises in the Word of God. Search for promises that apply to you. Meditate constantly on the promises you have chosen. Believe that God will bring these promises into manifestation in your life.

Whenever we're faced with adversity, *we should be consumed by Jesus Christ. Every aspect of our lives should revolve around His indwelling Presence.* We should lift Him up constantly in our thoughts, words and deeds. We should praise Him and thank Him continually. If we follow these instructions, we *will* walk in His victory and bring it into manifestation in our lives.

Unfortunately, some Christians struggle in an attempt to win a victory that *already has been won.* We should *walk* in the victory of Jesus Christ twenty-four hours a day. His magnificent victory belongs to us *every* day of our lives. We should "...hold fast and firm to the end our joyful and exultant confidence and sense of triumph in our hope [in Christ]" (Hebrews 3:6).

Our Father wants us to *hold fast and firm* when we're faced with problems. If we *know* we have victory over these problems, wouldn't we wait for manifestation of this victory with joy and confidence? We must believe we triumph in Christ!

This chapter is filled with several magnificent promises from God's Word. Go back and study each of these promises. Meditate on them constantly. Personalize these promises. Appropriate them for yourself.

Satan hates to see us react in this way. His only hope is in his ability to deceive us. We should refuse to allow Satan to steal the victory Jesus has provided for us. Our Father wants us to persevere at all times. In the next chapter, we'll look into the Word of God to see why Satan doesn't want us to persevere in faith.

Chapter 7

Satan Wants Us to Give Up

Satan doesn't want us to know the truth about the victory we have been given by Jesus Christ. Jesus wants us to fill our minds and hearts with truth from God's Word pertaining to His victory. Satan wants us to believe the lies he whispers into our ears. *"...he is a liar [himself] and the father of lies and of all that is false"* (John 8:44).

When we go through a season of adversity, we won't give up if we refuse to believe Satan's lies. If we know what God's Word says and if we stand in faith on it, we will be set free. Jesus said, *"...If you abide in My word [hold fast to My teachings and live in accordance with them], you are truly My disciples. And you will know the Truth and the Truth will set you free"* (John 8:31-32).

Whenever we're faced with problems, we must make a choice. Will we believe the lies of Satan and act accordingly? Or will we *abide* in God's Word and *believe* what it says? Will we always do our best to live our lives *in obedience to* the instructions in the Word of God? If we follow these instructions, *we will know the Truth and the Truth will set us free.*

Satan knows the power of Christians whose hearts are filled with God's Word and persevere in faith. Because of this, Satan does everything he can to get us to give up *before* we receive manifestation of the blessings our Father wants to give us. Satan wants to *steal* the victory Jesus has given to us. "The thief comes only in order to *steal* and *kill* and *destroy...*" (John 10:10).

Jesus doesn't want us to give in to Satan. The last part of this passage of Scripture explains the victory Jesus provided for us. Let's look at this verse of Scripture in its entirety. "The thief comes only in order steal and kill and destroy. *I came that they might have and enjoy life and have it in abundance (to the full, till it overflows)."* (John 10:10).

Jesus wants us to *enjoy life.* He has provided *abundantly* for us. We shouldn't allow Satan to steal from us, kill us and destroy us. Jesus *doesn't* want us to become discouraged and give up. Jesus explained His desire to the apostle Peter. He said, "Simon, Simon (Peter), listen! Satan has asked excessively that [all of] you be given up him [out of the power and keeping of God], that he might *sift* [all of] you like grain, but *I have prayed especially for you [Peter], that your [own] faith may not fail...*" (Luke 22:31-32).

Satan apparently is able to ask God for an opportunity to *sift* us. When grain is sifted, it is passed through a sieve which is a utensil with many small openings. A sieve is used to separate coarse and fine particles. When Satan tries to sift us, *he wants to separate us from our faith.*

Jesus warned His apostles that Satan wanted to sift them. He was particularly concerned about Peter. Jesus prayed especially for Peter that Satan wouldn't be able to separate him from his faith and that his faith would remain strong. *Jesus wants our faith to remain strong when Satan tries to "sift" us.*

When we go through a long, drawn out ordeal, Satan's evil spirits often whisper discouraging words into our ears.

When you're struggling, haven't you had thoughts like this rise up in your mind? "This is a hopeless situation. There is no way I can succeed. I'm going to give up."

Most of us have experienced this type of thinking when we have faced a severe problem or when we have gone through a frustrating delay. These thoughts often are not our own thoughts. They are put into our minds by Satan's evil spirits. Some Christians don't know or believe that Satan and his evil spirits are able to put thoughts into our minds. Satan and his evil spirits are much more effective if we don't realize what they're trying to do to us.

We must not underestimate Satan's ability to put thoughts into our minds. This process is so effective that Satan actually was able to persuade one of the apostles of Jesus Christ to betray Him. *"...Satan having already put the thought of betraying Jesus in the heart of Judas Iscariot..."* (John 13:2).

Did you ever wonder how an apostle of Jesus Christ could turn against Him? Judas lived with Jesus. He saw Him perform many miracles. He had experienced the love and compassion of Jesus Christ. Nevertheless, Judas turned against Jesus *because he allowed Satan to get into his mind.*

This passage of Scripture proves that Satan tries to influence our behavior. He has been attempting to influence people for six thousand years. Satan and his evil spirits try to put thoughts into our minds. They want us to dwell on these thoughts long enough so that they will drop from our minds down into our hearts. Then we often will act based upon what has gotten into our hearts.

When we go through a long, difficult ordeal, we should expect Satan's evil spirits to whisper lies into our ears. They want us to become discouraged and give up. We must not allow Satan to get leverage over us in this way.

God's Word says *we can "...keep Satan from getting the advantage over us; for we are not ignorant of his wiles and intentions"* (II Corinthians 2:11).

When Satan tries to discourage us, we must realize that we have been given victory over him and all of his evil spirits. Jesus said, *"Behold! I have given you authority and power to trample upon serpents and scorpions, and [physical and mental strength and ability] over all the power that the enemy [possesses]; and nothing shall in any way harm you"* (Luke 10:19).

This passage of Scripture is extremely powerful. Jesus Christ has given every Christian the authority and power to *trample upon Satan and his evil spirits.* The words "serpents and scorpions" refer to Satan and his evil spirits. Jesus has given us the physical and mental strength and the ability to put *all* of their attacks under our feet. If we persevere in faith, *nothing in any way can harm us!*

However, when we attempt to withstand Satan's attacks, we must know how to fight spiritual battles. *"...though we walk (live) in the flesh, we are not carrying on our warfare according to the flesh and using mere human weapons. For the weapons of our warfare are not physical [weapons of flesh and blood], but they are mighty before God for the overthrow and destruction of strongholds"* (II Corinthians 10:3-4).

When Satan attacks us, we can't shoot him with a gun. We can't stab him with a knife or hit him with our fists. We must not try to resist him with flesh and blood. We should realize the futility of attempting to fight spiritual warfare with human weapons. Instead, we should fight our battles with the mighty weapons God has given us.

God's Word tells us exactly what to do when Satan tries to put thoughts into our minds. *"...[we] refute* arguments and theories and reasonings and *every* proud and lofty thing that sets itself up against the [true] knowledge of God; and we lead *every* thought and purpose away captive into the obedience of Christ (the Messiah, the Anointed One)..." (II Corinthians 10:5)

If we refute something, we refuse to accept it. This passage of Scripture tells us that we can lead every thought *away* from what Satan is trying to tell us. We *can* bring *every* thought into *obedience* to Jesus Christ. If we couldn't do these things, God's Word wouldn't say we could.

Jesus Christ gave us a total victory. We shouldn't be afraid of Satan and his followers. "...*do not* [for a moment] be frightened or intimidated in *anything* by your opponents and adversaries, for such [constancy and fearlessness] will be a *clear sign* (proof and seal) to them of [their impending] destruction..." (Philippians 1:28).

When we persevere with faith in the face of every severe problem and refuse to give up, our faithful perseverance is very discouraging to Satan and his evil spirits. They attempt to intimidate us. They want us to be frightened by the problems we face. If we refuse to be frightened or intimidated, we give Satan and his followers a clear indication that we walk in faith in the unconditional victory Jesus Christ has given to us.

When Satan tries to defeat us, we must follow our Father's instructions. "...be vigilant and cautious *at all times*; for that enemy of yours, the devil, roams around like a lion roaring [in fierce hunger], seeking someone to seize upon and devour. *Withstand him; be firm in faith [against his onset — rooted, established, strong, immovable, and determined]*, knowing that the same (identical) sufferings are appointed to your brotherhood (the whole body of Christians) throughout the world" (I Peter 5:8-9).

Please underline or highlight the words *at all times*. We should *always* be on guard. We should expect Satan to come at us vigorously. We must stand up against Satan's attacks with strong, deeply rooted and established faith.

We need to realize that many other Christians are being attacked by Satan. Satan wants us to think we are the only ones who are suffering. He wants us to feel sorry for ourselves — to have a "pity party." We all have been given a victory over Satan. If we know what God's Word says and if we deeply believe God's promises we will refuse to give up.

God's Word is our spiritual ammunition. If we fill our hearts with it, Satan won't be able to wear us down. Instead, we will overcome him. "Is not My word like *fire* [that consumes all that cannot endure the test]? says the Lord, and like a *hammer* that breaks in pieces the rock [of most stubborn resistance]?" (Jeremiah 23:29).

Satan can't stand up against the power of the Word of God living in our hearts. Many Christians are familiar with the words "resist the devil and he will flee." However, Satan *will not flee* unless we obey the specific instructions given to us in this passage of Scripture. "*...be subject to God. Resist the devil [stand firm against him], and he will flee from you. Come close to God and He will come close to you...*" (James 4:7-8).

We can only resist Satan effectively if we're *subject to God*. When we're subject to God, we obey the instructions in His Word and we cheerfully yield control of our lives to the Holy Spirit. Satan is afraid of God. When we *draw close to God, He promises to come close to us. Satan will flee!*

Jesus Christ shed His blood so we could overcome Satan. No matter what Satan tries to do to us, we have been given the ability to overcome him through the shed

67

blood of Jesus Christ and by boldly speaking the Word of God. "...they have overcome (conquered) him by means of the *blood of the Lamb and by the utterance of their testimony...*" (Revelation 12:11).

We fight spiritual battles with our mouths. Our hearts are the storehouse for the spiritual ammunition contained in the Word of God. When we study and meditate continually on God's Word, we store up this precious spiritual ammunition. Whenever our hearts are filled with something, our heartfelt beliefs pour out of our mouths. Jesus said, "*...out of the fullness (the overflow, the superabundance) of the heart the mouth speaks*" (Matthew 12:34).

Whenever any of us are faced with a severe crisis, we will react based upon whatever we really believe in our hearts. We are instructed again and again to fill our hearts with the Word of God so that our thoughts, words and actions in a time of crisis will be based upon our Father's instructions to us.

Whenever we're engaged in a long and difficult spiritual battle, we should retaliate by doing the same thing Jesus did when Satan tried to wear Him down during His grueling forty day fast. Every time Satan tried to get at Jesus, He replied "*It is written*". Jesus then spoke specific Scripture references (see Matthew 4:1-10).

Imagine how weary you might be after fasting for thirty or thirty-five days on a forty day fast. How would you react if Satan kept hammering away at you in your weakened condition? Jesus wants us to follow His example. When we're faced with a severe problem, He wants us to *boldly speak the Word of God*. When we're under severe pressure, *our words should line up with God's Word.*

When Satan's evil spirits try to persuade us to give up, *they listen carefully* to the words that come out of our mouths. They want to hear us speak words that indicate they are getting into our minds and hearts. They *know* they have been successful if they hear words of discouragement coming out of our mouths. These words are music to their ears.

Our Father wants us to speak His Word boldly. We release God's power when we constantly speak His Word out of a faith-filled heart. Satan can't get at us when we follow these instructions. *"...by the word of Your lips I have avoided the ways of the violent (the paths of the destroyer)"* (Psalm 17:4).

At the beginning of this chapter, we saw that Satan's mission is to steal, kill and destroy. We can avoid the path of the destroyer when our hearts are filled with the Word of God and God's Word continually pours out of our lips. We will always emerge victorious in spiritual warfare if we follow our Father's instructions.

Every Christian has the responsibility of knowing what the Word of God says about the magnificent victory we have been given over Satan. Our minds and hearts should be filled with many Scripture references pertaining to this victory. When we boldly speak faith-filled words from God's Word, *we actually activate angels to work on our behalf!* "...you His angels, you mighty ones who do His commandments, *hearkening to the voice of His word*" (Psalm 103:20).

The atmosphere around us is filled with God's angels and Satan's fallen angels. We have just seen that we are able to give angels "marching orders" by the words we speak. On the other hand, we give Satan and his evil spirits power they cannot attain in any other way if the words that come out of our mouths are contrary to God's Word.

Satan is very persistent, but we should be more persistent. He can *only* stop us if we allow Him to *steal* the victory Jesus Christ won for us. We must persevere against the attacks of Satan. In the next chapter, I'll give practical examples as well as specific instructions from the Word of God telling us how to persevere.

Chapter 8

The Importance of Perseverance

I'd like to start this chapter with examples of people who persevered and succeeded. I'll start with an explanation of the benefits of perseverance in my own life. I *don't* do this to glorify myself. I only give these examples to illustrate how a person like myself with very little natural ability can succeed because of perseverance.

Before I knew anything about spiritual rebirth and the victory of Jesus Christ, I learned a lot about perseverance. While I was a child, I had to deal with several personal and family problems that my friends didn't have to face. I was inhibited by these problems and I became shy and withdrawn. When I graduated from high school, I was voted the most bashful person in my class.

By the grace of God I was able to attend college. I worked throughout high school and college to earn money. I didn't have an automobile or a driver's license until I was twenty-three years old. I walked almost everywhere I went. When I graduated from college I ranked in the bottom ten percent of my class.

After serving two years in the army, I went into the business world. I was overwhelmed by the skills and intelligence of many people I worked with. Because of my inferiority complex, I didn't see how I could possibly do as well as these people who obviously had much more ability than I did.

I didn't give up. It took many years, but ultimately I was able to enjoy a considerable amount of business success. As I look back, I don't believe this process was unusual. Most people reading this book know people without a lot of natural ability who persevered and succeeded.

Please think back to your class in high school or college. Did you have classmates with a great deal of natural ability who never have amounted to very much in the years since graduation? On the other hand, did you have classmates without much natural ability who have become quite successful over the years because they persevered and refused to give up? *I believe perseverance is much more important than talent.*

Because I enjoyed moderate success as an employee in the first ten years after I left the army, I became a self-employed businessman at the age of thirty-four. Our business struggled from the beginning. I was constantly in debt. I wasn't a Christian at that time and I knew virtually nothing about the Bible.

From the age of thirty-four to the age of forty-three, I was desperate because of the near failure of my business. Because of my financial problems, I continually read books about positive thinking and success. I also read many biographies of successful men and women who persevered throughout trials.

I read biographies of George Washington, Abraham Lincoln, Winston Churchill, Harry Truman and many others. I read about the Pilgrims and their amazing perseverance after they left England to come to America. I read many other accounts of great perseverance of the early settlers in this country. I did my best to apply the principles I learned from these books.

For approximately nine years I was able to survive because I saturated myself in books about positive thinking and because I constantly read biographies of successful people who persevered. I finally found myself on the verge of bankruptcy. There didn't seem to be any way out. I refused to give up. I disregarded the advice of my attorney and accountant to file bankruptcy.

At the age of forty-three I was at the end of my human ability. I didn't know where to turn. At that time a friend of mine told me about Jesus Christ. He said I could overcome the problems in my life if I asked Jesus to be my Saviour and if I walked each day in His victory. I asked Jesus that day to live in my heart. I immediately started to study and meditate continually on the Word of God.

I definitely would have failed if I had tried to keep going with my limited human strength and ability. The positive thinking books helped for awhile, but I finally realized that I needed much more. Day after day I saturated myself in the holy Scriptures. I wrote hundreds of pages of notes based upon what I learned from the Bible.

I mistakenly failed to attend a church during my first year as a Christian. My Father was gracious to me. I listened continually to Christian radio stations and I watched many Christian television programs. I loved to hear Christians give testimonies explaining how God brought them through seemingly impossible situations. I listened to many Christian cassette tapes that inspired me and enabled me to keep going.

By God's grace, I was able to persevere and succeed in business. I was able to keep going because I saturated myself in the Word of God. I refused to allow anything to distract me. I knew I was on the right track and I refused to be deterred. "...no longer be children, tossed [like ships] to and fro between chance gusts of teaching and wavering with every changing wind of doctrine..." (Ephesians 4:14).

I was able to persevere then and I'm able to persevere today by focusing continually on the promises in God's Word. This Bible study and meditation helps me to draw closer to the One Who made these promises. Our Father honors His children who have been broken and humbled and, as a result, study and meditate continually on His Word. "...*this is the man to whom I will look and have regard: he who is humble and of a broken or wounded spirit, and who trembles at My word and reveres My commands*" (Isaiah 66:2).

I believe our lives here on earth are similar to a marathon. Our Father isn't looking for flashy people who are fast starters. We don't succeed in the most difficult times of life because of human abilities. "...the race is *not* to the *swift* nor the *battle* to the *strong*..." (Ecclesiastes 9:11).

As I have studied God's Word over the years, I have become convinced that our Father is looking for *staying power*, not starting power. His eyes constantly search the earth looking for His children who dare to trust Him and refuse to give up. "...the eyes of the Lord run to and fro throughout the whole earth to show Himself strong in behalf of those whose hearts are blameless toward Him..." (II Chronicles 16:9).

As we go through the marathon of life, we can persevere through extremely difficult times by focusing continually upon Jesus Christ. "...*let us run with patient endurance and steady and active persistence the appointed course of the race that is set before us, looking away [from all that will distract] to Jesus, Who is the Leader and the Source of our faith [giving the first incentive for our belief] and is also its Finisher [bringing it to maturity and perfection]...*" (Hebrews 12:1-2).

I love this passage of Scripture. We are told that we each have to run the appointed course of the race. God had a plan for each of us when He formed us in our mother's womb. Each person is called upon by the Lord to run his or her lifetime marathon. Our Father wants us to run this race with *patient endurance and steady and active persistence.*

We all will come upon times in our lives when we can't go any farther with human ability. When we come to these times, our Father wants us to be patient. We must not allow our emotions to control us. Our Father wants us to endure, to be steady and to do our best. He wants us to let go and trust completely in Him.

We do this by looking away from everything that could distract us. Our Father doesn't want us to focus continually on the problems we face. Once we have identified our problems and acknowledged them, we should *turn away from the problems to focus continually on Jesus Christ.* He won a glorious victory over every problem we will ever face. *He will bring us safely across the finish line if we dare to trust completely in Him and absolutely refuse to give up.*

As we attempt to deal with the problems in our lives, many of us will be faced with obstacles that seem to be overwhelming. Jehoshaphat, the king of Judah, once faced an army that was extremely large and powerful. He said, "...we have *no might* to stand against this great company that is coming against us. *We do not know what to do, but our eyes are upon You*" (II Chronicles 20:12).

When we're faced with problems that seem to be overwhelming, we should do what Jehoshaphat did. Instead of giving up, *we should keep our eyes on the Lord at all times.* The Lord brought Jehoshaphat and his followers through to victory many years ago. He will bring us through our problems today if we refuse to focus on our problems *because our eyes are always on Him.*

Our Father promises to protect us and to keep us in perfect peace if we trust completely in Him. *"You will guard him and keep him in perfect and constant peace whose mind [both its inclination and its character] is stayed on You, because he commits himself to You, leans on You, and hopes confidently in You"* (Isaiah 26:3).

This is a magnificent promise. Are you going through a difficult ordeal? *Would you like God Himself to guard you and protect you? Would you like Him to keep you in perfect and constant peace? Our Father has promised these benefits to each of His children.*

However, this promise is *conditional.* God will *always* do His part, but *we must do our part.* Many people who are faced with adversity think about their problems continually. *We must not fall into this trap. We should keep our minds on God at all times.* If we are totally committed to Him, we'll *lean* on Him and place *all* of our hope in Him. We'll refuse to give up because we *trust completely* in Him.

The Bible gives us a wonderful example of this principle when it tells how Moses brought two million Israelites to the Red Sea. The Israelites faced a seemingly impossible situation. The Red Sea was in front of them. They were surrounded by mountains on both sides. Pharaoh and his mighty army were behind them. Moses refused to give up. *"...he never flinched* but held staunchly to his purpose and endured steadfastly as one who *gazed on Him Who is invisible"* (Hebrews 11:27).

As Moses led the Israelites out of Egypt, he refused to flinch. I mentioned previously that we flinch when we draw back from anything that is difficult or dangerous. Moses refused to draw back. He was single-minded. *He was able to endure because he constantly focused his attention on God — on Him Who is invisible.*

The Israelites needed the leadership of Moses because they focused constantly on the *problems* they faced. They were *terrified* when they saw the mighty army drawing close to them. "When Pharaoh drew near, the Israelites looked up, and behold, the Egyptians were marching after them; and *the Israelites were exceedingly frightened and cried out to the Lord*" (Exodus 14:10).

Instead of focusing on the problem, Moses trusted the Lord. "Moses told the people, *Fear not; stand still* (firm, confident, undismayed) and see the salvation of the Lord which *He will work for you today.* For the Egyptians you have seen today you shall never see again. *The Lord will fight for you, and you shall hold your peace and remain at rest*" (Exodus 14:13-14).

This passage of Scripture contains an important lesson for us. Instead of allowing fear to get inside of us, we should stand on our faith in the Lord. He will honor our faith. If we remain at peace and rest in the Lord, *He will fight our battles for us.*

The Lord urged Moses to encourage the Israelites. He told Moses to step out in faith and He gave him specific instructions telling him how to do this. The Lord said, "...Tell the people of Israel to go forward! Lift up your rod and stretch out your hand over the sea and divide it, and the Israelites shall go on dry ground through the midst of the sea" (Exodus 14:15-16).

God parted the Red Sea for Moses and the Israelites. Then, the same angel who parted the Red Sea went behind the Israelites and formed a cloud between them and the Egyptians. "...the Angel of God Who went before the host of Israel moved and went behind them; and the pillar of the cloud went from before them and stood behind them..." (Exodus 14:19).

The Egyptians couldn't see through the cloud. They were blinded and they didn't know what was happening in front of them. "Then Moses stretched out his hand over the sea, and the Lord caused the sea to go back by a strong east wind all that night and made the sea dry land; and the waters were divided. And the Israelites went into the midst of the sea on dry ground, the waters being a wall to them on their right hand and on their left" (Exodus 14:21-22).

When the Egyptians tried to follow the Israelites into the opening in the Red Sea, God closed down the opening and they were destroyed. "The waters returned and covered the chariots, the horsemen, and all the host of Pharaoh that pursued them; not even one of them remained" (Exodus 14:28).

If our loving Father was able to bring two million Israelites safely through the seemingly impenetrable waters of the Red Sea and He was able to destroy Pharaoh and the entire Egyptian army, *will you believe He can and will bring you safely through the problems you face?* Refuse to flinch. Focus your attention on the Lord at all times. Don't give up. Trust completely in God. "*...be steadfast and patient in suffering and tribulation...*" (Romans 12:12).

It's easy to give up. It isn't easy to be steadfast and patient in the midst of a long, trying ordeal. Our Father doesn't want us to waver. He wants us to trust Him. He wants us to be tenacious, single-minded, determined and unyielding.

Chapter 9

Persevere in the Will of God

We all have seen people who aren't Christians who have persevered and reached their goals. Many parents who refused to give up on their children have been rewarded for their perseverance. Inventors who have persisted in spite of persistent failures have been honored for their perseverance. I believe God, by His grace, rewards many people for their perseverance. However, I believe our Father *guarantees* to reward His children for perseverance when we find *His will* for our lives and *refuse to give up.*

Our Father has a specific plan for each of us. I believe the following statement He made to Jeremiah applies to every person. *"Before* I formed you in the womb I *knew* and *approved* of you [as My *chosen instrument]..."* (Jeremiah 1:5). God knows exactly what He wants to do with our lives. The Psalmist said, "Your eyes saw my unformed substance, and in Your book *all the days [of my life] were written before ever they took shape, when as yet there was none of them"* (Psalm 139:16).

We must believe in our hearts and profess with our mouths that Jesus Christ has paid the price for our sins. We must trust completely in Him for eternal salvation. If we do these things, we are reborn spiritually. We are recreated for a specific purpose. *"...we are God's [own] handiwork (His workmanship), recreated in Christ Jesus, [born anew] that we may do those good works which God predestined (planned beforehand) for us [taking paths which He prepared ahead of time], that we should walk in them [living the good life which He prearranged and made ready for us to live]"* (Ephesians 2:10).

This passage of Scripture explains *why* we were recreated when we were reborn spiritually. God has a plan for the remainder of our lives after we're born again. If He didn't, all Christians would go immediately to heaven after being reborn spiritually. God's Word says that our Father prepared in advance definite paths for each of His children to follow.

We must realize that *our lives are not our own.* Jesus died for us. He wants us to die to personal goals to live our lives for Him. *"...[if] One died for all, then all died; and He died for all, so that all those who live might live no longer to and for themselves, but to and for Him Who died and was raised again for their sake"* (II Corinthians 5:14-15).

We should devote our lives to carrying out God's plans. We should surrender control of our lives to God and give ourselves to Him to use as He desires. *"...offer and yield yourselves to God* as though you have been raised from the dead to [perpetual] life, and your bodily members [and faculties] to God, *presenting them as implements of righteousness"* (Romans 6:13).

The apostle Paul knew that we have to persevere when we attempt to fulfill God's plans for our lives. He said, *"...I press on* to lay hold of (grasp) and *make my own,* that for which Christ Jesus (the Messiah) has laid hold of me and made me His own" (Philippians 3:12). Paul was completely dedicated to do what Jesus Christ called him to do. *"...one thing I do [it is my one aspiration]; forgetting what lies behind and straining forward to what lies ahead..."* (Philippians 3:13).

Paul was so dedicated to carrying out God's plan for his life that he focused on it continually. Paul said, *"...the Holy Spirit clearly and emphatically affirms to me in city after city that imprisonment and suffering await me. But none of these things move me; neither do I esteem my life dear to myself, if only I may finish my course with joy and the ministry which I have obtained from [which was entrusted to me by] the Lord Jesus..."* (Acts 20:23-24).

Paul knew he would face severe adversity on many different occasions. He *never allowed* problems to move him. He *wasn't interested* in personal goals. Paul *was consumed by* the need to persevere to successfully complete the assignment Jesus gave to him.

Every Christian should have a consuming desire to fulfill God's plan for his or her life. Everything we think, everything we say and everything we do ideally should be dedicated to carrying out God's will for our lives. *"...aim at and pursue righteousness (all that is virtuous and good, right living, conformity to the will of God in thought, word, and deed)..."* (II Timothy 2:22).

We live in the last days before Jesus returns. Time is short. We shouldn't waste time chasing after selfish goals. *"Look carefully then how you walk! Live purposefully and worthily and accurately, not as the unwise and witless, but as wise (sensible, intelligent people), making the very most of the time [buying up each opportunity], because the days are evil. Therefore do not be vague and thoughtless and foolish, but understanding and firmly grasping what the will of the Lord is"* (Ephesians 5:15-17).

Jesus Christ is our example. During His earthly ministry, Jesus never concerned Himself with personal goals. He was completely dedicated to carrying out His Father's will. Jesus said, "...I *do not* seek or consult My own will [I have *no* desire to do what is pleasing to Myself, My own aim, My own purpose] but *only the will and pleasure of the Father Who sent Me*" (John 5:30).

So far in this chapter, I have attempted to explain the importance of finding God's will for our lives. Now, let's see *why it is so important to persevere* in carrying out the assignment we have been given. "...if this doctrine or purpose or undertaking or movement is of *human origin* it will *fail* (be overthrown and come to nothing); but *if it is of God, you will not be able to stop or overthrow or destroy them...*" (Acts 5:38-39).

God *doesn't* promise to honor our perseverance when we pursue *personal* goals. However, He promises that *nothing can stop us if we persevere in His will for our lives.* Christians should pray continually to ask God to reveal His will for their lives. When we know we are in the center of God's will, our faith should be unyielding. We should persevere continually. *We can't fail because God will not be denied in seeing His will carried out.*

Anyone who has read the Book of Job knows that Job went through some very difficult times. However, Job knew that nothing could stop God. "...Job said to the Lord, I know that *You can do all things, and that no thought or purpose of Yours can be restrained or thwarted*" (Job 42:1-2).

If we diligently seek to find and carry out God's will for our lives, *we have every right to believe God will honor our faith and perseverance.* We should *never* be concerned about anything that comes against us. *Nothing can stop God!* "...*who can resist and withstand His will?*" (Romans 9:19).

Sometimes it seems as if everything we are doing is in vain. Our Father knows what we are doing on His behalf. He wants us to persevere. "...my beloved brethren, *be firm (steadfast), immovable,* always abounding in the work of the Lord [always being superior, excelling, doing more than enough in the service of the Lord], *knowing and being continually aware that your labor in the Lord is not futile [it is never wasted or to no purpose]*" (I Corinthians 15:58).

This passage of Scripture has encouraged me many times in the ministry the Lord has given me. On several different occasions I have been in an position where it seemed as if there was no way I could accomplish the assignment I knew the Lord had given to me. However, even though I couldn't see any way out, I persevered and kept going because I was certain I was doing what God called me to do.

Our Father knows exactly what each of His children is going through. He *will* reward us for our perseverance. "...God is *not* unrighteous to *forget* or *overlook* your labor and the love which you have shown for His name's sake in ministering to the needs of the saints (His own consecrated people), as you still do" (Hebrews 6:10).

We must not allow obstacles to deter us. Our Father wants us to focus continually on His plan for our lives. We should be single-minded and keep moving forward at all times. "Let your eyes look right on [*with fixed purpose*], and let your gaze be *straight* before you" (Proverbs 4:25).

No matter how difficult it might be to carry out God's will for our lives, we must understand that *God is completely dependable. He will not let us down.* "...those who are ill-treated and suffer *in accordance with God's will* must do right and commit their souls [in charge as a deposit] to the One Who created [them] *and will never fail [them]*" (I Peter 4:19).

When I'm faced with adversity as I attempt to carry out God's will, I'm often comforted because I know God has provided a multitude of angels to help me. *"...He will give His angels [especial] charge over you to accompany and defend and preserve you in all your ways [of obedience and service]"* (Psalm 91:11).

Our Father has given specific angels a definite assignment to stay with us, to defend us and to preserve us in *everything* we do on His behalf. Our Father also has given us the power of His Word to live in our hearts. He has provided the Holy Spirit to guide and encourage us. We have been given *everything* we need to carry out God's will for our lives. *We must persevere. We must not give up!*

Chapter 10

We Depend Upon Almighty God

When we're committed to carrying out God's will for our lives, we should expect to go through seasons of adversity. Our Father wants us to trust Him completely. God is *omnipotent* — He is all powerful. He is *omniscient* — He knows everything. He is *omnipresent* — He is able to be in many different places at the same time. *Our Father is in complete control of every situation.* "...the Lord our God the Omnipotent (the All-Ruler) *reigns!*" (Revelation 19:6).

Our Father is more than sufficient to bring each of His children through any problem we will face. *We must not allow our problems to seem bigger than God.* Too many of us magnify the problems in our lives when we should be exalting Almighty God and trusting completely in Him. We cannot afford to focus on our problems. We must draw close to our Father.

If we have a distant relationship with our Father, our problems will seem to be immense. God will seem to be small, vague and distant. However, if we continually draw close to our Father, we'll strengthen the belief deep down inside ourselves that He *really is* much greater than any problem we will face.

Sometimes our Father allows our problems to get to the point where we must turn to Him. He wants each of

His children to trust totally in Him. *"I will say of the Lord, He is my Refuge and my Fortress, my God; on Him I lean and rely, and in Him I [confidently] trust!"* (Psalm 91:2).

Many times we will be faced with problems that seem to be absolutely impossible to solve. When *every* door seems to be closed and there doesn't seem to be *any* way out, we must realize that God can bring us through if we keep our faith in Him and refuse to give up. *"...With men this is impossible, but all things are possible with God"* (Matthew 19:26).

Whenever a situation looks hopeless, I believe we should say something like this. "Dear Father, I can't see *any* way out of this problem. However, I know *You* can see *many* solutions to this problem. I trust completely in You, dear Father. I know You *will* bring me safely through. *I will not give up* because my faith in You is strong and unwavering."

God's ways are much higher than our ways. We must not limit Him. We don't have to fight every battle by ourselves. He is with us every hour of every day. He wants to help us. *"...with us is the Lord our God to help us and to fight our battles..."* (II Chronicles 32:8).

Too many of us want to give up *because we're trying to fight battles our Father doesn't want us to fight.* Many times we do our best to solve a problem, but nothing we do seems to work. We must not give up. We should persevere because we trust God to fight for us. *"...the battle is not yours, but God's"* (II Chronicles 20:15).

Most Christians have heard the story of David and Goliath. However, when we're faced with severe problems, it's helpful to have much more than just "head knowledge" of this magnificent story. Let's look into the Word of God to receive inspiration from this wonderful example of God's strength prevailing in the midst of a seemingly impossible situation.

As you read the story of David and Goliath, I suggest that you take any severe problem you might face and call it your "Goliath." If you know you can't solve your problems with your limited human ability, I suggest that you look at yourself as David.

This story tells about a battle between the Israelites and the Philistines. The Israelites looked fearfully at a mighty Philistine warrior named Goliath. This giant was *almost ten feet tall*! "And a champion went out of the camp of the Philistines named Goliath of Gath, whose height was six cubits and a span *[almost ten feet]*" (I Samuel 17:4).

The Israelites looked at an opponent who was almost twice as tall as they were. In addition to his size, Goliath was covered with bronze armor. He wore a bronze helmet on his head and he carried a mighty spear. "Goliath stood and shouted to the ranks of Israel, Why have you come out to draw up for battle? Am I not a Philistine, and are you not servants of Saul? Choose a man for yourselves and let him come down to me. If he is able to fight with me and kill me, then we will be your servants; but if I prevail against him and kill him, then you shall be our servants and serve us" (I Samuel 17:8-9).

The Israelites were terrified when they heard what this giant said. When they looked at him and saw how immense and powerful he was, they turned and fled because they were afraid. "And all the men of Israel, when they saw the man, *fled from him, terrified*" (I Samuel 17:24).

Our Father doesn't want us to react to our problems in this manner. We shouldn't allow the imagined consequences of the problems we have to get inside of us.

People who do this become terrified and run away from their problems. Instead of reacting this way to the "Goliaths" in our lives, we should emulate David.

David was a young boy who happened to be present in the camp of the Israelites because his father had told him to take bread and cheese to his brothers who were Israelite soldiers. Just as David arrived with these provisions, he heard Goliath's threat. *David wasn't afraid. "David said to Saul, Let no man's heart fail because of this Philistine; your servant will go out and fight with him"* (I Samuel 17:32).

Can you imagine how amazed Saul must have been to hear this young boy speaking these words immediately after his mighty warriors had fled in terror? "And Saul said to David, You are *not* able to go to fight against this Philistine. *You are only an adolescent*, and he has been a warrior from his youth" (I Samuel 17:33).

David refused to be discouraged because he *didn't* trust in his inadequate human strength. He trusted the Lord. "David said, The Lord Who delivered me out of the paw of the lion and out of the paw of the bear, *He will deliver me* out of the hand of this Philistine. And Saul said to David, *Go, and the Lord be with you!"* (I Samuel 17:37).

King Saul sent David to fight Goliath because he knew David was trusting completely in the Lord. Can you imagine how Goliath must have laughed when he saw this teenaged boy come out to face him? "And when the Philistine looked around and saw David, *he scorned and despised him*, for he was but an adolescent, with a healthy reddish color and a fair face" (I Samuel 17:42).

David *stood up* to his mighty opponent. *"Then said David to the Philistine, You come to me with a sword, a spear, and a javelin, but I come to you in the name of the*

Lord of hosts, the God of the ranks of Israel, Whom you have defied. This day the Lord will deliver you into my hand, and I will smite you and cut off your head..." (I Samuel 17:45-46).

David's response to the giant tells us exactly how our Father wants each of us to react when we're faced with a seemingly impossible situation. *We don't have to trust in human resources.* David said, "...the Lord saves *not* with sword and spear; for *the battle is the Lord's, and He will give you into our hands"* (I Samuel 17:47).

This statement teaches us that God isn't depending upon our human ability, strength and wisdom. Please underline the words *the battle is the Lord's.* These words tell us to trust the Lord and to let Him fight for us instead of thinking we have to do everything ourselves.

David had so much faith in the Lord that he did exactly the opposite of what his countrymen did. Instead of running away from Goliath as the other Israelites did, David did just the opposite. When the giant moved toward David, *he ran toward the giant.* "When the Philistine came forward to meet David, *David ran quickly toward the battle line to meet the Philistine"* (I Samuel 17:48).

When David ran toward Goliath, *he stepped out in faith.* God honored his faith. "David put his hand into his bag and took out a stone and slung it, and it struck the Philistine, sinking into his forehead, and he fell on his face to the earth. So *David prevailed* over the Philistine with a sling and with a stone, and struck down the Philistine and slew him. But *no sword* was in David's hand" (I Samuel 17:49-50).

This story isn't a fairy tale. *This event actually took place.* A young, adolescent boy with a slingshot and a stone actually defeated a mighty giant who was covered with seemingly impenetrable armor. Our Father wants each of His children to do likewise. We must believe He will fight our seemingly impossible battles for us and give us the victory.

Our Father won't let us down. *"...[God] Himself has said, I will not in any way fail you nor give you up nor leave you without support. [I will] not, [I will] not, [I will] not in any degree leave you helpless nor forsake nor let [you] down (relax my hold on you)! [Assuredly not!]"* (Hebrews 13:5).

Notice that the words *I will not* are used *four* different times in this one verse of Scripture. Repetition in the Bible is used to emphasize a point. Our Father wants us to be very *certain* He won't leave us in a helpless situation. He is very *emphatic* about this promise.

If you are going through a difficult ordeal and it seems as if God doesn't even know you exist, please meditate on this passage of Scripture. Personalize it. Appropriate these promises from Your Father to you. Our Father will *never* fail us or leave us without support. *We aren't helpless because God is with us!*

Our Father loves us more than we can comprehend. He promises to bring us through *every one* of our problems *if* we will trust in His love for us. *"...amid all these things, we are more than conquerors and gain a surpassing victory through Him Who loved us"* (Romans 8:37).

Let's examine this passage of Scripture carefully. First, please notice the italicized word *all*. Our Father doesn't promise us victory in *some* of our problems or *most* of our problems. If we do our best to obey the instructions in God's Word, to yield control of our lives to the Holy Spirit and to find and carry out God's will for our lives, our Father promises us victory in *all* of our problems!

Next, please notice the italicized words *more than conquerors* and *surpassing victory*. Our Father doesn't just promise that we will conquer our problems. He says we will be *more* than conquerors. He will give us *a surpassing victory* because the victory Jesus Christ won for us *surpasses* any problem we will face!

This victory will be brought into manifestation in our lives if we dare to trust in God's love for us. *Nothing* can separate us from our Father's love. *"...I am persuaded beyond doubt (am sure) that neither death nor life, nor angels nor principalities, nor things impending and threatening nor things to come, nor powers, nor height nor depth, nor anything else in all creation will be able to separate us from the love of God which is in Christ Jesus our Lord"* (Romans 8:38-39).

No problem, no matter how difficult it may seem to be, should separate us from a deep, abiding and continuous consciousness of our Father's love for us. Love is the greatest power in the universe because God and love are the same. *"...God is love"* (I John 4:8).

This passage of Scripture doesn't say God has love for us. It says God *is* love. God's love for us is sufficient to bring us through *every* problem. "Love bears up under *anything* and *everything* that comes, is ever ready to believe the best of every person, its hopes are fadeless under all circumstances, and *it endures everything [without weakening]. Love never fails..."* (I Corinthians 13:7-8).

We can persevere against any problem if our lives are centered around God's love for us. If we truly center our lives around God's love and if His love within us is extended to other people, *we won't give up. God never fails. God is love. Love never fails.*

This chapter is filled with encouraging promises from the Word of God. If you're faced with severe problems, I urge you to "saturate" yourself in these passages of Scripture. Soak them up. Personalize them. Fill your mind and heart with these precious promises. We *can* depend on *every* promise in the word of God. *"God is faithful (reliable, trustworthy, and therefore ever true His promise, and He can be depended on)..."* (I Corinthians 1:9).

Chapter 11

Persevere in the Strength
of the Lord

Our Father loves us. Because He loves us, He has made provisions enabling us to persevere in *His strength*. There is *not one place* in the Bible where we're told to rely completely upon our human ability. Christians who do this make a big mistake. "He who leans on, trusts in, and is confident of his own mind and heart *is a [self-confident] fool...*" (Proverbs 28:26).

I like the amplification of the original Greek in this passage of Scripture. We're *foolish* when we're self-confident. No matter how much natural ability any person might have, we must learn to trust in God and *not* in ourselves. "...a mighty man is *not* delivered by [his] much strength" (Psalm 33:16).

God created us. He knows how inadequate we are. His Word warns us against trusting in human ability "*Not that we are fit (qualified and sufficient in ability) of ourselves to form personal judgments or to claim or count anything as coming from us, but our power and ability and sufficiency are from God*" (II Corinthians 3:5).

However, no matter how gifted any person might be, no one has what it takes to persevere through some spiritual problems that cannot be solved through human ability. We open the door to Satan if we trust completely in our inadequate human abilities. "...*Cursed* [with *great evil*] is the *strong man* who trusts in and relies on *frail man*, making weak [human] flesh his arm, and whose mind and heart turn aside from the Lord" (Jeremiah 17:5).

From a worldly perspective, it is beneficial to be strong, self-confident and self-reliant. Many courses are taught on the subject of self-confidence. Jesus didn't trust in Himself. He said, "I am able to do *nothing* from Myself [independently, of My own accord - *only* as I am taught by God and as I get His orders]..." (John 5:30).

I have often thought that one of the biggest liabilities we can have is to have a lot of God-given "natural ability." From a worldly perspective, beauty queens, successful athletes and people in positions of leadership are often revered. God's ways are *different* from the ways of the world. God says that strong and self-reliant people are *cursed with great evil.*

We must realize how frail and inadequate all human ability is. We make a gigantic mistake if we trust in human ability and turn away from the Lord. We are nothing without Jesus Christ. Jesus said, "...apart from Me [cut off from *vital union* with Me] you can do *nothing*" (John 15:5).

When we're in the midst of a long, drawn out ordeal *we must turn towards the Lord, instead of turning toward our human ability.* Human patience and perseverance often will not be sufficient. Only God can provide the steadfast endurance we need. *It is "...God Who gives the power of patient endurance (steadfastness)..."* (Romans 15:5).

Where do we get the patient endurance to keep going when everything seems lost? Where do we get the steadfastness to "hang in there" when there doesn't seem to be any hope? We don't have these qualities in ourselves. They come from God.

Many people give up when they get to the point where they know their human strength and ability are woefully inadequate. Our Father promises to give us the strength we need to persevere. *"The Lord will give [unyielding and impenetrable] strength to His people..."* (Psalm 29:11).

God's strength is *so great* that we won't ever have to yield to *any* problem *if we really believe* His strength is available to us. God's strength is impenetrable. No problem is greater than His strength. *"...be strong in the Lord [be empowered through your union with Him]; draw your strength from Him [that strength which His boundless might provides]"* (Ephesians 6:10).

We can only appropriate God's strength through our union with Him. Christians who have an "arm's length" relationship with God can't appropriate His strength. If we want to utilize God's strength, we must have a close relationship with Him. We must draw close to Him continually.

If we do this, we'll get to the point where our trust in God is much greater than our faith in ourselves. *Why* would we ever trust in ourselves if we can trust in God? He reigns over the entire universe. His strength is available to *every one of His children*. *"...You reign over all. In Your hands are power and might; in Your hands it is to make great and to give strength to all."* (I Chronicles 29:12).

Please underline or highlight the last word in this passage of Scripture. When God says *all*, He includes *you* in this statement! Your Father has promised to give you the strength you need to deal with the problems you face. He has promised to make each of His children great. If we honestly believe what God says, we'll never give up!

The apostle Paul had an intimate relationship with Timothy. Paul knew Timothy was weak in many areas. He encouraged him to keep going in the strength of Jesus Christ. Paul said, "...my son, be strong (*strengthened inwardly*) in the grace (spiritual blessing) *that is [to be found only] in Christ Jesus*" (II Timothy 2:1).

We should be encouraged to realize the magnificent strength that is available to us. No Christian will ever be faced with any problem that is too great for the strength of the Lord Jesus Christ. *"I have strength for all things in Christ Who empowers me [I am ready for anything and equal to anything through Him Who infuses inner strength into me; I am self-sufficient in Christ's sufficiency]"* (Philippians 4:13).

This passage of Scripture is my favorite. I can't begin to tell you how many times Philippians 4:13 has strengthened me during the past twenty years. On dozens of occasions when I have been faced with difficult problems, I have opened my mouth and boldly spoken this promise. *When my ears hear my lips speaking this magnificent promise, I am always strengthened on the inside because our faith is always strengthened when our ears hear our mouths boldly speaking the Word of God.* "...faith comes by *hearing* [what is told]..." (Romans 10:17).

Instead of feeling sorry for ourselves because of our human weakness and inadequacy, we should *rejoice* that we are so weak and inadequate. When we're faced with difficult problems, our Father wants us to open our mouths and *admit* how weak we are. Then, in the same breath, we should speak boldly of the strength that is available to us through the Lord. *"...let the weak say, I am strong [a warrior]!"* (Joel 3:10).

No matter how weak we are in human ability, we must realize that the strength of Jesus Christ is more than sufficient to meet every need. *"...for My strength and power are made perfect (fulfilled and completed) and show themselves most effective in [your] weakness. Therefore, I will all the more gladly glory in my weaknesses and infirmities, that the strength and power of Christ (the Messiah) may rest (yes, may pitch a tent over and dwell) upon me!"* (II Corinthians 12:9).

We should be *glad* that we're weak in human strength because the strength of Jesus Christ can *only* be manifested in our lives *when we know how weak we are.* "So for the sake of Christ, I am *well pleased* and *take pleasure in* infirmities, insults, hardships, persecutions, perplexities and distresses; *for when I am weak [in human strength], then am I [truly] strong (able, powerful in divine strength)"* (II Corinthians 12:10).

Many human beings allow fear to get into their hearts because they know how inadequate they are to deal with the problems they face. We must not allow fear to get inside of our minds and hearts. Fear has an enervating effect upon us. It eats away at us if it gets inside of us. If our lives are truly centered around the Lord, *we won't give in to fear.* "...The Lord is the Refuge and Stronghold of my life — *of whom shall I be afraid?"* (Psalm 27:1).

Why would we ever be afraid of anything if we really believe God lives inside of us? If we continually draw close to Him, we won't be afraid. "Fear not [there is nothing to fear], for I am with you; do not look around you in terror and be dismayed, for I am your God. I will strengthen and harden you to difficulties, yes, I will help you..." (Isaiah 41:10).

Before I was a Christian I read the words "I am with you always." During the dark and dreary years before I asked Jesus to live in my heart, I often repeated the words "I am with you always" when I was faced with a severe problem. I didn't really know what those words meant, but it comforted me to think that God was always with me.

Now that I have become a Christian and understand this principle I am comforted even more by God's presence. I believe the most important thing any Christian can do is to have a continual consciousness — twenty-four hours a day, seven days a week, fifty-two weeks a year — that Jesus Christ lives in our hearts. *"...it is no longer I who live; but Christ (the Messiah) lives in me..."* (Galatians 2:20).

Jesus Christ has won a total victory over every problem we have had, every problem we have now and every problem we ever will have. He isn't concerned in the slightest with His ability to solve the problems that seem so perplexing to us. Jesus wants us to trust Him to solve our problems instead of trying to do everything ourselves. "God is our Refuge and Strength [mighty and impenetrable to temptation], *a very present and well-proved help in trouble"* (Psalm 46:1).

If we take refuge in God and if we really do trust in His strength, the problems in our lives won't be able to penetrate into our minds and hearts. Satan won't be able to tempt us if we place all of our hope in the strength of God. Our Father will help His children who trust completely in Him and refuse to give up. He knows exactly what to do to bring us safely through every problem. "...the Lord *knows how to* rescue the godly out of temptations and trials..." (II Peter 2:9).

When we're too weak to keep going, our hearts should *sing with joy* because we *know* the strength of the Lord will bring us through. *"The Lord is my Strength and my [impenetrable] Shield*; my heart trusts in, relies on, and confidently leans on Him, *and I am helped; therefore my heart greatly rejoices*, and with my song will I praise Him" (Psalm 28:7).

The Psalmist went through many difficult ordeals. He trusted in the Lord's strength and his heart rejoiced. We should follow his example. Instead of reacting negatively to problems, our Father wants us to be quiet and calm deep down inside of ourselves. *"...in quietness and in [trusting] confidence shall be your strength"* (Isaiah 30:15).

This passage of Scripture tells us the *two* sources of spiritual strength - *quietness* and *confidence*. If we really want to appropriate the Lord's strength, we must remain calm and quiet whenever we face severe problems. We block the Lord's strength if we panic. However, *if we remain calm because of our confidence in Him, this quietness and confidence will enable us to appropriate His strength.*

Some people have a "pity party" when they're faced with severe problems. They have a severe case of the "poor me's." Our Father doesn't want us to be depressed. He wants us to *rejoice* when we're faced with difficult trials. *"...be not grieved and depressed, for the joy of the Lord is your strength and stronghold"* (Nehemiah 8:10).

God always rejoices. No problem is too great for Him. If we really believe this, we won't ever feel sorry for ourselves. Instead, we'll draw strength from the joy of the Lord. His strength is able to invigorate us. If we believe this, we should seek His strength continually. "Seek the Lord and His strength; yearn for and seek His face and to be in His presence *continually!*" (I Chronicles 16:11).

Our Father doesn't want us to be in His presence occasionally. We should have a deep yearning to be constantly in His presence. If we yearn for something, *we long for it*. We're *consumed* by this desire. "Seek, inquire of and for the Lord, and *crave Him and His strength* (His might and inflexibility to temptation); seek and require His face and His presence *[continually] evermore*" (Psalm 105:4).

This passage of Scripture tells us what we must do when we need to endure and persevere. If we seek the Lord at all times and crave a close relationship with Him, His strength will sustain us. If we are in the Lord's presence, *nothing* can hurt us. He will bless us when we trust in His strength. *"Blessed (happy, fortunate, to be envied) is the man whose strength is in You..."* (Psalm 84:5).

Christians who don't know how to appropriate the strength of the Lord aren't much better off here on earth than unsaved people who can only go through adversity trusting in human strength. If you're faced with a problem you can't solve, *please realize that God isn't depending on you to solve the problem. We must not try to do God's work for Him.*

This chapter is filled with Scripture references promising that the Lord will strengthen us. If your strength isn't sufficient, don't give up. Meditate continually on these passages of Scripture. They will strengthen you.

Chapter 12

The Holy Spirit Will Help
Us to Persevere

When our human ability and strength are insufficient to successfully carry out God's will for our lives, we should know that the Holy Spirit will give us the strength to persevere. "...*be strengthened and reinforced with mighty power in the inner man by the [Holy] Spirit [Himself indwelling your innermost being and personality]*" (Ephesians 3:16).

We don't have to struggle as unsaved people do. Our Father has given us the Holy Spirit to help us carry out the goals He has for us. ".. we have *not* received the spirit [that belongs to] the world, but *the Holy Spirit Who is from God...*" (I Corinthians 2:12).

When we must persevere in the face of seemingly impossible obstacles, we must *know* deep down in our hearts that *God Himself lives inside of us and that He can and will help us when we're too weak to keep going in our strength*. "*...the [Holy] Spirit comes to our aid and bears us up in our weakness...*" (Romans 8:26).

When Jesus came to earth to carry out His earthly ministry, the Holy Spirit actually led Jesus into the desert to be tested by Satan. "Then Jesus, full of and controlled by the Holy Spirit, returned from the Jordan and was led in [by] the [Holy] Spirit for (during) forty days in the wilderness (desert), where He was tempted (tried, tested exceedingly) by the devil..." (Luke 4:1-2).

Why did the Holy Spirit lead Jesus into the desert to be tempted exceedingly by Satan? I believe He did this to prepare Jesus for His earthly ministry. We also must expect to face severe adversity as we seek to carry out God's will for our lives. After completing this forty day ordeal through the power of the Holy Spirit, Jesus was ready to begin His earthly ministry. "Then Jesus went back *full of and under the power of the [Holy] Spirit* into Galilee, and the fame of Him spread through the whole region round about" (Luke 4:14).

Jesus successfully completed His earthly ministry the same way our Father wants each of us to carry out His assignment for our lives. If we yield control of our lives to the Holy Spirit and if we're filled with and controlled by Him, Satan *won't* be able to stop us. *No* worldly problems can stop us because "...He Who lives in you is *greater* (mightier) than he who is in the world" (I John 4:4).

Satan is the god of this world. Jesus triumphed over Satan when He rose from the dead. The battle has been won. *The power of the Holy Spirit in us is greater than any circumstance we'll face in this world.* No matter how difficult our problems might seem to be, we *don't* have to solve them with our limited ability. "...*Not* by might, *nor* by power, but *by My Spirit...*" (Zechariah 4:6).

Our Father wants us to study and meditate on His Word continually. If we fill our minds and hearts with the Word of God, the Holy Spirit will help us to live according to God's instructions. "...*I will put My Spirit within you and cause you to walk in My statutes, and you shall heed My ordinances and do them*" (Ezekiel 36:27).

If the Holy Spirit had the power to raise Jesus from the dead, He certainly has the power to overcome *any* problem we'll ever experience. "...if the Spirit of Him Who raised up Jesus from the dead dwells in you, [then] He Who raised up Christ Jesus from the dead will also restore to life your mortal (short-lived, perishable) bodies through His Spirit Who dwells in you" (Romans 8:11).

When we're so weary we don't believe we can keep going, the Holy Spirit *will* give us the energy and desire to do whatever God wants us to do. We must realize that the Holy Spirit "...*is all the while effectually at work in you [energizing and creating in you the power and desire], both to will and to work for His good pleasure and satisfaction and delight*" (Philippians 2:13).

The Holy Spirit doesn't work in us occasionally — He works in us *all the while*. He is always at work inside of us. He works *effectually* — His work produces great results. The Holy Spirit *energizes* us. He provides the energy we need to do whatever He wants to do in us and through us. He gives us the *power* we need. He also gives us the *desire* to do whatever He wants us to do.

The apostle Paul was noted for his perseverance. Paul refused to give up in the face of many seemingly impossible situations. He knew the Holy Spirit would give him the energy to keep going. Paul said, "For this I labor [unto weariness], *striving with all the superhuman energy which He so mightily enkindles and works within me*" (Colossians 1:29).

We don't have what it takes to persevere under great pressure. All human beings have many "leaks" that show up during times of severe adversity. Because of this fact, it is vitally important for all Christians to "...*ever be filled and stimulated with the [Holy] Spirit*" (Ephesians 5:18).

The *only* way we can be *filled* and *stimulated* with the Holy Spirit is to be *emptied* of our own selfish desires. All Christians are here on earth to carry out God's will. We must turn away from our desires so the Holy Spirit can fill us with His will for our lives.

The Holy Spirit knows the assignments our Father has given to each of us. If we utilize His power and ability, we *will* be successful in carrying out these assignments. The Holy Spirit *"...by (in consequence of) the [action of His] power that is at work within us, is able to [carry out His purpose and] do superabundantly, far over and above all that we [dare] ask or think [infinitely beyond our highest prayers, desires, thoughts, hopes, or dreams]..."* (Ephesians 3:20).

Our Father has a definite plan for each of our lives. The Holy Spirit works inside of us to carry out the assignments our Father has given to us. *If we'll get out of the way and trust Him, He can and will do in our lives much, much more than we dare to ask or think.*

We must dare to trust the Holy Spirit. He knows exactly what He wants to do in our lives. He doesn't want us to attempt to do His work for Him. *"Do not quench (suppress or subdue) the [Holy] Spirit..."* (I Thessalonians 5:19).

If we yield control of our lives to the Holy Spirit and trust completely in Him, there is *no limit* to what He can and will do in us and through us. He is able to superabundantly guide us to carry out God's will for our lives to a degree that is infinitely beyond anything we would dare to ask or think. He will reveal God's plan to us if we will quiet our minds each day with the sincere desire to hear His voice.

Satan tries to influence us to become discouraged when we're faced with a situation that seems to be hopeless.

Satan's evil spirits whisper into our ears telling us to give up. *Nothing is hopeless to the Holy Spirit.* *"May the God of your hope so fill you with all joy and peace in believing [through the experience of your faith] that by the power of the Holy Spirit you may abound and be overflowing (bubbling over) with hope"* (Romans 15:13).

Would you like to be overflowing with hope? God's Word tells us this blessing is available to us. This passage of Scripture refers to our Father as *the God of your hope.* We are told that He will fill us with joy and peace if we have faith in the power of the Holy Spirit.

If the Holy Spirit truly is in control of our lives, we won't give up because He will sustain us. Problems that seem insurmountable to us become opportunities to listen to the voice of the Holy Spirit. He is God. He sees every circumstance in our lives from an eternal perspective. He will give us the power to persevere.

I know I am weak and inadequate. When I go through a difficult ordeal, I often open my mouth and say something like this: "Dear Father, I *don't* have the strength and ability to keep going in the face of these problems. I *thank You* for making the magnificent ability of the Holy Spirit available to me. Holy Spirit, *I trust You completely.* I yield control of my life to You. I pray in the name of Jesus Christ asking You to release Your power to solve these problems I face. Thank You, Holy Spirit."

When we go through the grueling marathon of life and it seems as if we can't possibly reach the finish line, we can persevere because the energy, power, strength and ability of the Holy Spirit are available to us. If we'll wait on Him and trust completely in Him, He will bring us safely through every season of adversity.

Chapter 13

Wait for the Lord

We have seen that God will guide us and strengthen us when we're unable to keep going with our human ability. When we're tired, we have been given the ability to partake of His unlimited energy. When we don't know what to do, Our Father knows exactly what must be done. *"...The everlasting God, the Lord, the Creator of the ends of the earth, does not faint or grow weary; there is no searching of His understanding"* (Isaiah 40:28).

God created everything and everyone on the earth. Nothing can cause Him to become weary. When you and I are worn out, God has unlimited energy and stamina. When we can't see any possible solution to our problems, He knows many ways to solve these problems. We can't begin to comprehend what God knows and how much He understands.

I have often been faced with problems that seemed to be hopeless. *God is faithful.* If we refuse to give up and persevere because we trust in Him, He *will* bring us safely through our problems. Our Father usually doesn't do this the way we think He will or when we think He will do it, but we can depend on Him.

Our Father will give us the power to keep going when we're weary. When we're weak, He can increase our strength to a level beyond our comprehension. *"He gives* power to the faint and weary, and to him who has no might He increases strength [causing it to multiply and making it to abound]" (Isaiah 40:29).

Sometimes our problems are so severe that even young men with all of the energy of youth wouldn't be able to keep going. God still promises to give us the strength to persevere. "Even youths shall faint and be weary, and [selected] young men shall feebly stumble and fall exhausted; but those who wait for the Lord [who expect, look for, and hope in Him] shall change and renew their strength and power; they shall lift their wings and mount up [close to God] as eagles [mount up to the sun]; they shall run and not be weary, they shall walk and not faint or become tired" (Isaiah 40:30-31).

I believe this passage of Scripture is one of the most important passages in the Bible for Christians who need to persevere. Imagine being in a situation that requires so much endurance that even the most physically fit young people in the world don't have the strength to keep going. When we find ourselves in such a situation, we are instructed to wait for the Lord.

What does it mean to wait for the Lord? I like the amplification in this passage of Scripture. It says that to wait for the Lord is to expect, look for, and hope in Him. When we can't keep going because of inadequate human strength or ability, we should expect the Lord to help us. He wants us to look for His assistance. We must not give up hope. We should place all of our hope in the Lord.

If we persevere and wait for the Lord, the situation will change. God will renew our strength and power. If we stay close to Him, we'll be like eagles who have the power to spread their wings and soar over the top of a storm. We'll be able to persevere without being weary, faint or tired.

God never gives up. There is no place in God's Word that tells us to give up. No matter how difficult our problems might seem to us, we must wait for the Lord. *"Wait and hope for and expect the Lord; be brave and of good courage and let your heart be stout and enduring. Yes, wait for and hope for and expect the Lord"* (Psalm 27:14).

When we're faced with a long, grueling season of adversity, Satan and his assistants try to persuade us to give up hope. Our Father wants us to place *all* of our hope in Him. We should *expect* Him to help us. He wants us to *endure patiently* because we have *complete confidence* in Him.

Whenever we face *any* problem, our Father wants us to do the *best* we can with the human ability He has given us. *"Whatever* your hand finds to do, do it with *all your might..."* (Ecclesiastes 9:10). Once we've done our best, we can't do any more. When we have done our best, we have only *one* alternative — to continually wait for God and to *expect* Him to help us. *"...wait [expectantly]* for your God *continually!"* (Hosea 12:6).

While we're waiting, we should spend time with the Lord each day. We should study and meditate on His Word. We should pray and worship Him continually. If we do these things on a daily basis, we *won't give up hope*. We'll *expect* the Lord to answer our prayers. *"...I will wait with hope* and *expectancy..."* (Micah 7:7).

Whenever we're faced with seemingly impossible problems, our Father wants us to trust so much in Him that we'll wait as long as He requires. *We never wait alone.* The Holy Spirit will help us while we wait for God's answer. *"...through the [Holy] Spirit's [help], by faith anticipate and wait for the blessing..."* (Galatians 5:5).

We should *expect* the Holy Spirit to help us. Instead of giving up, our faith should be strong enough to anticipate the blessing God has for us. Our thoughts, words and actions while we wait should clearly indicate our faith that God will bless us.

We shouldn't give in to our emotions while we wait. Instead, we should rest in the Lord while we're waiting. "...he who has once entered [God's] rest also *has ceased from [the weariness and pain] of human labors...*" (Hebrews 4:10).

When we enter into God's rest, we *stop* worrying and hurrying and trying to make things happen. Many people give up because they believe they have to solve their problems with their abilities. *We can only enter into God's rest when we cease from the weariness and pain of human labor.*

We must admit that we don't have what it takes to persevere. We should be constantly aware of God's presence. He is with us every step of the way. He wants us to rest in Him because we know He is always with us. "...*the Lord said, My Presence shall go with you, and I will give you rest*" (Exodus 33:14).

The Psalmist David was mature in the Lord. He trusted completely in the Lord and waited for Him. David said, "My soul, wait *only* upon God and silently submit to Him; for my hope and expectation *are from Him.* He *only* is my Rock and my Salvation; He is my Defense and my Fortress, *I shall not be moved*" (Psalm 62:5-6).

Please note that the word *only* is used twice in this passage of Scripture. Waiting for the Lord often is our *only* alternative. When we don't have any other option, we should silently submit to God. When we wait for Him, *all* of our hope and expectation should be in Him. We *should not be moved by our problems.*

If we truly trust the Lord, we'll be very consistent while we wait. Immature people go through many emotional ups and downs. Mature Christians should be calm, cool and collected when they face problems. They are able to persevere because they trust the Lord. *"...be calm and cool and steady, accept and suffer unflinchingly every hardship..."* (II Timothy 4:5).

God is always fair. If we wait for Him and refuse to give up, He *will* pour out blessings upon us. *"...the Lord is a God of justice. Blessed* (happy, fortunate, to be envied) are *all* those who *[earnestly] wait for Him,* who *expect* and *look* and *long for Him* [for His victory, His favor, His love, His peace, His joy, and His matchless, unbroken companionship]!" (Isaiah 30:18).

Our Father promises to bless *all* of His children who earnestly wait for Him. This word *all* includes you! If your problems seem to be so difficult that no one can solve them, realize that God has promised to bless you if you wait for Him. He will never let you down!

We're instructed to wait for the Lord *earnestly.* We should be very serious, determined and intense while we wait for the Lord. We should *expect* Him and *look for* Him. We should long for a close relationship with Him.

Our Father will bless us if we wait for Him. His love for us is much greater than we can comprehend. If we really expect Him to help us, we will be able to walk in His peace and His joy while we wait for Him. "The Lord is *good* to those who *wait hopefully* and *expectantly* for Him..." (Lamentations 3:25).

The Word of God repeatedly says the Lord is good to us when we refuse to give up hope. Our Father promises to bring us through if we *obey* His instructions and have *deep faith* that He will solve our problems. *"Wait for and expect the Lord and keep and heed His way, and He will exalt you..."* (Psalm 37:34).

This passage of Scripture gives us additional instruction on how to wait for the Lord. Once again, we see the familiar instructions to wait for and expect the Lord. While we're waiting, we should do our best to obey the instructions in His Word. If we expect the Lord to help us and if we live our lives according to His instructions, He *will* lift us above our problems.

God is in complete control. We'll never be disappointed if we wait for Him. No matter how bad our problems might seem to be, we won't be ashamed if we keep our eyes on the Lord and refuse to give up because we fully expect Him to bring us through. *"...I am the Lord; for they shall not be put to shame who wait for, look for, hope for, and expect Me"* (Isaiah 49:23).

This chapter is filled with promises from God's Word telling us what our Father will do if we wait for Him because we trust Him. In the next chapter, we'll look into the Word of God for detailed instructions telling us *how* to build ourselves up while we're waiting for the Lord to answer our prayers.

Chapter 14

We Must Build Ourselves Up While We Wait

We should work diligently at strengthening our faith while we're waiting for God to answer our prayers. If we do this, we won't waver. Our faith will enable us to stop the attacks of Satan and his evil spirits. "Lift up over *all* the [covering] shield of *saving faith*, upon which you can quench *all* the flaming missiles of the wicked [one]" (Ephesians 6:16).

This passage of Scripture is very encouraging. It says we are able to withstand *all* of the missiles Satan fires at us. Are you going through a difficult time? Is it hard for you to persevere? Is Satan trying to wear you down? Underline or highlight the word *all* in this passage of Scripture. This passage of Scripture applies to *you* and the problems *you* are going through.

If we keep our faith strong, we'll be able to persevere and bring into manifestation the victory Jesus Christ won for us. However, we can't persevere if our faith is shallow. Christians who don't have deeply rooted faith will ultimately give up. "*...they have no real root in themselves, and so they endure for a little while...*" (Mark 4:17).

When we go through the storms of life, we are very much like trees in a hurricane. I have looked at trees that were ripped out of the ground by a hurricane. These trees had the most shallow roots. If we want to endure the storms of life, our faith and perseverance must be *deeply rooted* in the Word of God.

One of the best ways to build ourselves up when we're going through severe problems is to feed ourselves the spiritual food of God's Word each day. In the natural realm, we need to eat good, wholesome food to provide the energy we need. In the spiritual realm, we must feed ourselves good spiritual food to provide the faith to persevere.

The Word of God is our spiritual food. If we feed it to ourselves continually when we go through difficult times, it will build us up spiritually. "...I commend you to *the Word of His grace* [to the commands and counsels and promises of His unmerited favor]. *It is able to build you up and to give you [your rightful] inheritance* among all God's set-apart ones (those consecrated, purified, and transformed of soul)" (Acts 20:32).

We haven't earned the right to the thousands of precious promises in God's Word. Our Father has given us His Word through His grace. This passage of Scripture tells us that the Word of God *is able to build us up* so that we will be able to receive the inheritance God has provided for His children who set themselves apart by dedicating their lives entirely to Him.

If we want to build ourselves up we must be *purified* as a result of the constant cleansing of God's Word. Our souls should be *transformed* because they are constantly renewed from feeding God's Word into our minds and hearts.

Many years ago anointed men of God wrote the holy Scriptures to give us the encouragement we need to endure and persevere today. "For whatever was thus written in *former days* was written for our *instruction*, that by [our *steadfast* and *patient*] *endurance* and the *encouragement* [drawn] from the Scriptures we might *hold fast to and cherish hope*" (Romans 15:4).

Isn't it interesting to realize that God made provisions thousands of years ago for His Word to provide us the instruction we need today? If we continually fill our minds and hearts with the holy Scriptures, *we will be encouraged. We'll receive power to endure steadfastly and patiently. If we hold fast to these promises we won't give up hope.*

I can tell you from many years of experience that it isn't easy to study and meditate continually on the Word of God. I have gone through long seasons of time where I built myself up day after day in the Word of God. No matter how tired I was, I did this every day because I knew how important it was. We must be willing to pay a price when we study and meditate on God's Word.

If you're going through a difficult time, you must have a strong determination to build yourself up spiritually. Make up your mind to pay the price of studying and meditating on the Word of God *each and every day. "...Though our outer man is [progressively] decaying and wasting away, yet our inner self is being [progressively] renewed day after day"* (II Corinthians 4:16).

I love this passage of Scripture. We're told that our bodies progressively decay and waste away. In the world today, many people try to camouflage the aging process with wigs, hair coloring, makeup, girdles, etc. *We can only deal with the aging process from the inside out, not from the outside in.*

We should renew our minds on a daily basis at every age, but it is *especially important* to do this as the aging process accelerates. As our bodies decay more and more, *we must build ourselves up on the inside.* This renewal should be progressive. It must be done *day after day*. We can't persevere during difficult seasons in our lives if we only build ourselves up occasionally. We must be consistent. *"...be constantly renewed in the spirit of your mind [having a fresh mental and spiritual attitude]..."* (Ephesians 4:23).

Once again, God's Word instructs us to renew our minds constantly. If we want to stay fresh in our minds and in our hearts, we must build ourselves up continually. When we go through difficult times, we need fresh spiritual food every day.

We should renew our minds constantly so we won't think the way Satan wants us to think. *We can turn away from the ways of the world by forcusing constantly on God. "...set your minds and keep them set on what is above (the higher things), not on the things that are on the earth"* (Colossians 3:2).

I'd like to pause here to ask you, the reader of this book, to take a little quiz. I have asked the questions I'm about to ask to dozens of audiences throughout the United States and Canada. I have found that only ten percent to twenty percent of the Christians in the audience know the correct answer to the following important questions.

The word "success" is mentioned only *once* in the Bible. *Do you know* the *only* place in the Bible where the word "success" is mentioned? *Do you want to be successful in God's eyes*? If so, *do you know* the *three specific things* God's Word instructs us to do if we want to be successful and prosperous in everything we do?

You will find the answers to these questions in the following passage of Scripture. We must know, understand and apply these spiritual principles to persevere during the difficult seasons in our lives. *"This Book of the Law shall not depart out of your mouth, but you shall meditate*

*on it day and night, that you may observe and do according
to all that is written in it. For then you shall make your
way prosperous, and then you shall deal wisely and have
good success"* (Joshua 1:8).

I'd like to comment on the last part of this passage of
Scripture first. God says, "...*then you* shall make your way
prosperous, and *then you* shall deal wisely and have good
success." Our Father has given us specific instructions on
how to receive His prosperity, wisdom and success, but
this promise is *conditional*. We must do our part. *Then*
the Lord will do His part.

Let's look at the three specific instructions our Father
has given us. God gave these instructions to Joshua shortly
after Moses died and Joshua ascended to the position of
leadership of millions of Israelites. The *same* instructions
apply to each of us today.

I prefer to explain this passage of Scripture by
explaining the second principle first — to *meditate day
and night* upon the Word of God. *We renew our minds by
studying God's Word. I believe the Word of God drops
from our minds down into our hearts when we meditate
on it day and night.*

When we meditate on God's Word we "chew" and
"digest" the spiritual food contained in the Word of God.
When I meditate upon a passage of Scripture, I personalize
it. I put my name in the promise I'm meditating upon. I
reflect on the meaning of this passage of Scripture
throughout the day and night. I turn the Scripture over
and over in my mind, looking at it from many different
angles. I absorb everything I can from each passage of
Scripture.

Next, Joshua 1:8 says that God's Word *shouldn't
depart from our mouths*. We should speak the Word of
God constantly. Jesus told us in Matthew 12:34-35 that

the words that flow out of our mouths are based upon what we have stored up in our *hearts*. When we continually meditate on God's Word, we fill our hearts with the holy Scriptures. When our *hearts* overflow with the Word of God, the words from our *mouths* will line up more and more with God's Word.

Finally, Joshua 1:8 tells us *to observe and do according to all that is written* in the Word of God. If we study and meditate continually on God's Word, we program it into our minds and hearts. This process is similar to programming a computer. If we program God's Word into our minds and hearts continually we will *obey* its instructions. *If we follow each of the instructions from Joshua 1:8, we will be able to persevere successfully and prosper in everything we do.*

Satan and his evil spirits try to get at us through our minds so they can get down into our hearts. They know that our hearts are the key to our lives. If we constantly meditate on God's Word and fill our *hearts* with its supernatural power, *we will be able to persevere* against the attacks of Satan and his evil spirits. "*...the Word of God is [always] abiding in you (in your hearts), and you have been victorious over the wicked one*" (I John 2:14).

If you want to be able to persevere against the attacks of Satan, ask yourself if the Word of God constantly abides in your heart. If we build our hearts up *continually*, we *will* be able to persevere in the midst of severe pressure. "*Comfort* and *encourage* your hearts and *strengthen* them [make them *steadfast* and keep them *unswerving*] in every good work and word" (II Thessalonians 2:17).

God's Word gives us several specific instructions telling us exactly what our Father wants us to do to build ourselves up spiritually. "*Receive*, I pray you, the law and instruction from His mouth, and *lay up His words in your heart.* If you *return* to the Almighty [and *submit* and *humble* yourself before Him], *you will be built up...*" (Job 22:22-23).

This promise, like many other promises in the Bible, is a *conditional* promise. If we want to be built up spiritually, we must obey the specific instructions our Father has given us in this passage of Scripture.

First we are told to *receive instruction* from God. We do this by *filling our hearts* continually with the Word of God. We must *return to God* by turning away from personal desires to focus completely on Him. We must *submit to God* and *humble ourselves* before Him. If we follow these instructions, our hearts will be built up. Our words will line up with God's Word.

We have seen previously in Psalm 103:20 that words coming out of our mouths that are aligned with God's Word activate angels to work on our behalf. Conversely, words that deny the victory of Jesus Christ give Satan and his evil spirits spiritual power they cannot get in any other way. *We must understand the power of our words.* "How *forcible* are words of straightforward speech!..." (Job 6:25).

When we go through a long season of adversity, we should build ourselves up daily by speaking the Word of God out of faith-filled hearts. Every word we speak should indicate our faith in the Lord. "...*let us hold fast our confession [of faith in Him]*" (Hebrews 4:14).

When Satan and his evil spirits try to entice us to give up, we can fight back with the words we speak. If our hearts are overflowing with the Word of God, powerful and encouraging words from the holy Scriptures will pour out of our mouths. These faith-filled words will deliver us from the attacks of Satan. "...the mouth of the upright shall *deliver* them..." (Proverbs 12:6).

When we go through a difficult time, Satan wants us to react emotionally to our problems. *Our Father wants us to react based upon the promises in His Word.* He wants us to persevere by holding tightly on to His Word until the victory of Jesus Christ is manifested in our lives. "...these are [the people] who, hearing the Word, *hold it fast* in a just (noble, virtuous) and worthy heart, *and steadily bring forth fruit with patience"* (Luke 8:15).

Would you like to be able to *hold fast* during a prolonged season of adversity? Do you want to be able to *steadily bring forth fruit with patience?* Make the decision to hold tightly on to the Word of God. Your life could depend upon this. *"Take firm hold of instruction, do not let go; guard her, for she is your life"* (Proverbs 4:13).

Our faith must not waver. If we focus continually on God's precious promises and speak these promises constantly, we release spiritual power. *"...let us seize and hold fast and retain without wavering the hope we cherish and confess and our acknowledgment of it, for He Who promised is reliable (sure) and faithful to His word"* (Hebrews 10:23).

This passage of Scripture summarizes everything we have discussed in this chapter. When we go through adversity, we need to *seize* the promises in the Word of God. When we seize something, we take hold of it forcefully and hang on to it tightly. If we continually *hold fast* to God's Word while we go through a season of adversity, *our faith will not waver. We won't give up hope.* Our hearts will be filled with the encouragement of the Holy Scriptures. Our mouths will confess the glorious promises our Father has given us in His Word.

God is completely reliable. We can depend upon every promise in the Bible. Instead of focusing on our *problems,* we should focus constantly on the *promises* our Father has given us. If we do this, we will be strong spiritually. We will be able to persevere. *"The strong spirit of a man sustains him in bodily pain or trouble..."* (Proverbs 18:14).

This chapter is filled with Scripture references telling us how to build ourselves up while we wait on the Lord. I hope these wonderful promises will encourage you as they have encouraged me. In the next chapter, we'll look into God's Word to learn how to stand fast and persevere when we're faced with difficult problems.

Chapter 15

Stand on the Word of God

We have learned how to do the best we can with our human ability and then to build ourselves up spiritually, to rest in the Lord and to trust Him as we wait for His answer to our prayers. For many years I have focused on the following passage of Scripture whenever I was faced with a problem that was too difficult for me to handle. *"...having done all [the crisis demands], to stand [firmly in your place]"* (Ephesians 6:13).

Whenever we're faced with a crisis situation, we should do our very best to solve the problems we face. Once we have done our best, we should *stand in faith* that we share in the victory of Jesus Christ. The word "stand" is a military word. When an army moves forward and takes a certain amount of ground, they try to hold on to this ground. *"...hold fast what you have..."* (Revelation 3:11).

Jesus Christ has given us victory over every problem. We should hold fast because we trust completely in Him. Our Father wants us to stand just as an army stands. No matter what problems we face — a financial problem, a family problem, a health problem or a problem in any other area, we should *stand* boldly on our faith in the Lord.

We must not allow Satan to rob us of the magnificent victory Jesus has won for us. We should stand firmly in place because we *know* this victory has been given to us. "*...in [your] faith* (in your strong and welcome conviction or belief that Jesus is the Messiah, through Whom we obtain eternal salvation in the kingdom of God) *you stand firm*" (II Corinthians 1:24).

We're able to stand against the attacks of Satan because we know Jesus is the Messiah. If we're able to trust Jesus for eternal life in heaven, we certainly can trust Him to bring us through any problems we face here on earth. Jesus has given us victory over death and He has given us victory in every aspect of our lives on earth. We can stand firmly based upon our faith in this victory. "*...Christ has made us free [and completely liberated us]; stand fast then,* and do *not* be hampered and held ensnared and submit again to a yoke of slavery [which you have once put off]*" (Galatians 5:1).

We must place our total faith in Jesus. He won't let us down. He will honor our faith and perseverance. "*...he who believes in Him [who adheres to, trusts in, and relies on Him] shall not be put to shame nor be disappointed in his expectations*" (Romans 9:33).

Are you faced with a seemingly unsolvable problem? Open your mouth and say, "*I will not back up.* I don't care what the situation looks like. I *stand in faith* on the promises in God's Word. Jesus Christ has given me a total and unconditional victory. I refuse to give up."

Unfortunately, some Christians allow Satan to steal the victory Jesus Christ has provided for us. Some of us have faith for awhile, but we don't stand in faith *long enough.* If our faith in the Lord is strong enough, we'll stand firmly in place no matter how long it takes to receive the manifestation of His victory. *If we really believe we have the victory, why would we ever give up?*

When everything is going wrong, we should draw closer to God. We can *only* stand firmly in place when we're going through severe adversity if we have a *close* relationship with God. "...the people who *know their God* shall prove themselves *strong* and shall *stand firm* and do exploits [for God]" (Daniel 11:32).

Would you like to stand firm and do great things for God? Do you want to be able to appropriate His strength whenever you face a difficult problem? God's Word says that people who *know their God* are able to remain strong and stand firmly in place and do exploits for God.

We can't stand firmly in place against a difficult problem if we only have a casual "arm's length" relationship with God. It is very important to draw close to Him each day. When we go through difficult times, it is imperative to set aside time every day to study and meditate on the Word of God. We should worship the Lord and praise Him continually. We should pray constantly.

Also, whenever we're faced with difficult problems, we should join faith with *other Christians*. We should ask our brothers and sisters to stand with us in faith. "...you are *standing firm* in *united spirit* and purpose, striving *side by side* and contending with a *single mind* for the faith of the glad tidings (the Gospel)" (Philippians 1:27).

Our Father wants us to be single-minded in our faith in His Word. He wants His children to stand firm in united faith. When we know other Christians are going through a season of adversity, we should reach out *constantly* to them with encouragement. "...(admonish, urge, and encourage) one another *every day*..." (Hebrews 3:13).

Tremendous spiritual power is released when two or more Christians *stand together* in strong faith. *Jesus Christ joins with us* when we stand together in His name. Jesus said, "For wherever two or three are gathered (drawn together as My followers) in (into) My name, *there I AM in the midst of them*" (Matthew 18:20).

We can't stand against the attacks of Satan unless our faith is strong. We must have a deep conviction in the victory we have been given and stand courageously in faith. "*...stand firm in your faith* (your conviction respecting man's relationship to God and divine things, keeping the trust and holy fervor born of faith and part of it). Act like men and be courageous..." (I Corinthians 16:13).

Christians will face many problems, but Jesus has given us victory over *every problem*. God doesn't promise to deliver us from *some* of our problems. If we consistently do our best to obey the instructions in His Word, we have every right to believe He will deliver us from *every* problem. "Many evils confront the [consistently] righteous, but *the Lord delivers him out of them all*" (Psalm 34:19).

This chapter is filled with instructions telling us how to stand in faith when we're faced with difficult problems. If you are going through a season of adversity, go back over this chapter with a pen or a highlighter. Highlight or underline every place in this chapter where the word *stand* is used. Go back over each passage of Scripture and meditate on it continually. *God's Word will help you to stand firmly in faith against the problems you face.*

Chapter 16

Get Up - Don't Stay Down!

Life isn't easy. We all can expect to be knocked down many times. However, our Father wants us to *get up*. Satan has learned from many years of experience that he can knock some people down and they'll stay down. Because he has been successful doing this, Satan continues to knock people down. *We must not stay down!*

All Christians are soldiers in the army of Jesus Christ. When soldiers are engaged in a war, they know they will go through difficult times. The apostle Paul told Timothy, *"Take [with me] your share of the hardships and suffering [which you are called to endure] as a good (first-class) soldier of Christ Jesus"* (II Timothy 2:3).

We must be realistic. We all are called to endure a certain amount of hardship in our lives. Jesus is our Commander-in-Chief. *We please Him when we persevere in the face of adversity.* "No soldier when in service gets entangled in the enterprises of [civilian] life; his aim is to *satisfy* and *please* the one who enlisted him" (II Timothy 2:4).

We must not give up when we face problems in life. We please Jesus when we stand boldly in faith against these problems. Jesus wants us to endure as soldiers who have been given an unconditional victory by the One Who enlisted us in His army.

Anyone who has studied history knows that victorious armies often lose battles before they ultimately emerge victorious. I'm old enough to remember World War II. The situation looked very grim in the months immediately following the Japanese attack on Pearl Harbor. However, the tide eventually turned and the Allied Forces won victory in the Pacific. This same pattern was repeated on the European front. The Allied Forces didn't give up because they lost some early battles. They persevered and they won the war.

This same principle applies to us. *We may lose some battles, but we'll win the war if we refuse to give up.* We must not surrender just because we get knocked down a few times. We might *bend*, but we *shouldn't break*. We might *feel* like giving up, but we *must not give in* to these feelings.

Have you ever read the story of the life of Abraham Lincoln? This great Christian man lost many battles, but he refused to be defeated. Imagine how Abraham Lincoln must have felt as he went through the following events in his life:

YEAR	EVENT
1831	*Failed* in business
1832	*Defeated* for the Legislature
1833	*Failed again* in business
1834	Elected to the Legislature
1835	Fiancee *died*
1836	Suffered a *nervous breakdown*
1838	*Defeated* for Speaker
1840	*Defeated* for Elector
1843	*Defeated* for Land Officer
1844	*Defeated* for Congress
1846	Elected to Congress
1848	*Defeated* for Congress

1855	*Defeated* for Senate
1856	*Defeated* for Vice President
1858	*Defeated* for Senate
1860	Elected President

Please go back and read through each of these defeats and failures. I have listed thirteen defeats, but Abraham Lincoln persevered to win three important victories. Try to imagine how easy it would have been for Abraham Lincoln to give up. He was knocked down many times, but *he refused to stay down.*

Abraham Lincoln once said, "When you come to the end of your rope, *tie a knot in it and hang on.*" He also said, "My great concern is *not* whether you have failed, but whether you are *content* with your failure."

The life of Abraham Lincoln has been an inspiration to many people. The apostle Paul was another wonderful example of someone who persevered through severe trials. He once said, "We are hedged in (pressed) on *every* side [troubled and oppressed in *every* way], *but not cramped or crushed*; we suffer embarrassments and are perplexed and unable to find the way out, *but not driven to despair*; we are pursued (persecuted and hard driven), *but not deserted [to stand alone]*; we are struck down to the ground, *but never struck out and destroyed...*" (II Corinthians 4:8-9).

This passage of Scriptures gives us a summation of the severe adversity Paul faced. If you would like to do a detailed study of the problems Paul went through during his ministry, carefully study Paul's epistles (Romans through Philemon) and search for the many examples of the severe problems he faced. You will be encouraged by Paul's perseverance.

The earthly ministry of Jesus Christ gives us another magnificent example of perseverance. Any Christian who is faced with difficult times should read through the four gospels (Matthew, Mark, Luke and John) to see how Jesus continually persevered in the face of severe problems. Jesus should be our example in every area of life.

Meditate on the ordeal Jesus went through in the Garden of Gethsemane. Jesus told the apostles who were with him that He was deeply grieved. "...He began to *show grief* and *distress* of mind and was *deeply depressed.* Then He said to them, My soul is *very sad* and *deeply grieved,* so that I am *almost dying of sorrow...*" (Matthew 26:37-38).

Go back and read over these words. Realize that Jesus Christ actually said these things. *Aren't you glad that Jesus persevered and didn't give up?* Because of His perseverance, we can live eternally in heaven and also partake of His victory while we live here on earth. Jesus wants us to persevere just as He persevered.

We must be realistic. We will be knocked down on many occasions. On one occasion when Joshua laid on the ground discouraged, the Lord spoke to him. The same instructions apply to us today. "The Lord said to Joshua, *Get up! Why* do you lie thus upon your face?" (Joshua 7:10).

When we're knocked down, we don't have to trust completely in our own strength. The Lord promises to *help us* to get back up on our feet. "Though he falls, he shall *not* be utterly cast down, for *the Lord grasps his hand in support and upholds him"* (Psalm 37:24).

When we're knocked down, we must realize that Jesus lives inside of us. He lies on the ground with us. He will help us to get up. He *doesn't* want us to be depressed and give up. "*Arise* [from the depression and prostration in which circumstances have kept you — rise to a new life]! *Shine* (be radiant with the glory of the Lord..." (Isaiah 60:1).

Jesus doesn't want us to be victims of the circumstances in our lives. He has given us victory over every circumstance. We must not allow circumstances to cause us to become so depressed that we lie prostrate on the ground. We should *arise* from our problems and *shine radiantly* with the glory of the Lord.

Satan's evil spirits rejoice when a Christian is knocked down. They whisper into our ears trying to pull us into their darkness. They want us to be gloomy. Our Father wants us to turn away from the darkness and arise and *come into His light. "Rejoice not against Me, O my enemy! When I fall, I shall arise; when I sit in darkness, the Lord shall be a light to me"* (Micah 7:8).

Can you visualize Satan's evil spirits rejoicing when Christians have been knocked down? We should tell them to *stop rejoicing.* If we're knocked down, we *must not* identify with the darkness of Satan. *The Lord's light will shine into our lives if we get up and persevere because we trust in Him.*

Satan is extremely persistent. Christians should be *more persistent.* Satan can knock unsaved people down and they may ultimately quit because their strength runs out. *Christians should always get up because we can depend upon Jesus.* "...a righteous man *falls seven times and rises again*, but the wicked are *overthrown* by calamity" (Proverbs 24:16).

When we're knocked down, our Father wants to help us. When it looks as if we're about to sink, we should turn to "...God, Who *comforts* and *encourages* and *refreshes* and *cheers* the depressed and the sinking..." (II Corinthians 7:6).

This chapter contains a lot of information that will encourage us to *get up* if we're knocked down. In the next chapter, we'll study God's Word to learn the importance of praying continually whenever we go through difficult battles.

Chapter 17

Persevere in Prayer

We have seen how to build ourselves up spiritually and how to stand on God's Word while we're waiting on the Lord. We have seen that God wants us to get up when we're knocked down. Whenever we're faced with adversity, our Father wants us to be very patient. He also wants us to pray constantly. "...be *steadfast* and *patient* in suffering and tribulation; *be constant in prayer*" (Romans 12:12).

There are two primary reasons why we don't receive answers to prayer. We don't receive because we *don't ask* or because we ask with a *wrong motive.* "...You do not have, because you *do not ask.* [Or] you do ask [God for them] and yet fail to receive, because you ask with *wrong purpose and evil, selfish motives.* Your intention is [when you get what you desire] to spend it in sensual pleasures" (James 4:2-3).

When we pray with a motive we believe is approved by our Father, we can be *certain* He hears us *every* time we pray. "And this is the *confidence* (the assurance, the privilege of boldness) which we have in Him; [*we are sure*] that if we ask *anything* (make any request) according to His will (in agreement with His own plan), *He listens to and hears us*" (I John 5:14).

In addition to hearing all prayers according to His will, *we also can be certain that our Father will answer all of these prayers.* "And if (since) we [positively] know that He listens to us in whatever we ask, *we also know [with settled and absolute knowledge] that we have [granted us as our present possessions] the requests made of Him"* (I John 5:15).

We should always do our best to live in obedience to the instructions in God's Word. These instructions are our Father's general will for all of His children. We also should pray continually seeking God's specific will for our individual lives. If we follow these instructions, we *know* God hears our prayers.

We also *know* that we have *as our present possessions* the answer to our prayers. God answers prayers that are made according to His will at the very moment we pray. However, we often must persevere for a period of time before these answers are brought into manifestation. *If we know we have an answer from God, why would we ever give up?* "*...whatever you ask for in prayer, having faith and [really] believing, you will receive"* (Matthew 21:22).

Please review the passages of Scripture on the previous pages. Do you believe God does what He says He will do? *As you study these passages of Scripture, do you have any doubt that your Father hears you when you pray according to His will and that He definitely will answer your prayer requests?*

If we really want our prayers answered, we should draw closer to Jesus while we wait. Every aspect of our lives should be centered around Him. While we wait for the answers to our prayers to be brought into manifestation, we also should fill our hearts continually with the Word of God. Jesus said, "*If you live in Me [abide vitally united to Me] and My words remain in you and continue to live in your hearts, ask whatever you will, and it shall be done for you"* (John 15:7).

Jesus wants us to *live* in Him. We should *abide vitally united* to Him. We should stay close to Jesus at all times, but it is especially important to stay close to Him when we go through a season of adversity. Also, Jesus said that His words should *continue* to live in our hearts. We should feed ourselves spiritually on a daily basis. Christians who are close to the Lord on an ongoing basis and Christians whose hearts are filled with the Word of God can ask whatever they will, knowing that God will answer.

We must *persevere* in our prayers. *Our Father wants us to pray continually from our hearts. "...The earnest (heartfelt, continued) prayer of a righteous man makes tremendous power available [dynamic in its working]"* (James 5:16).

If we want to release the enormous power of God to receive manifestation of the answer to our prayers, we must pray *earnestly*. Our prayers should be *passionate, intense and fervent. The dynamic power of God is available to His children who pray with faith and refuse to give up!*

We must pray continually in the midst of a prolonged season of adversity when God doesn't seem to be answering our prayers. Satan and his evil spirits often try to stop the manifestation of answers to our prayers. When we pray fervently, we usually are engaged in spiritual warfare. Satan and his followers know the power of continual, fervent prayer. They do everything they can to persuade us to give up when it seems as if our prayers aren't being answered.

One of the best examples of the necessity for perseverance in prayer is in our prayers for unsaved loved ones. Satan knows he will live eternally in the lake of fire.

He wants *everyone* to join him in his eternal misery. "...the devil who had led them astray [deceiving and seducing them] was hurled into *the fiery lake* of burning brimstone, where the beast and false prophet were; and they will be *tormented day and night forever* and ever (through the ages of the ages)" (Revelation 20:10).

Satan hates to see people reborn spiritually. When this happens, Satan and his followers don't give up. They want the other members of our families to live eternally with them in the lake of fire. They do everything they can to prevent these people from receiving Jesus Christ as their Saviour.

Sometimes it seems as if our family members will never come to Christ. *We must persevere in our prayers for the salvation of other people.* When we do this, we fight each day for their eternal future. We should continually ask our Father to draw every person we're praying for to receive salvation. Jesus said, *"No one is able to come to Me unless the Father Who sent Me attracts and draws him and gives him the desire to come to Me..."* (John 6:44).

We *can't force* other people to become Christians. However, we can *pray continually and fervently* that God will reach down from heaven to draw these people to Him and give them the desire to ask Jesus Christ to be their Saviour. *Every person who has been reborn spiritually is drawn by God Himself.* We must not give up on these prayers!

When we pray for the salvation of other people, for our finances, our health or anything else, we must be willing to fight in the spiritual realm for the answer to our prayers. Satan tries to wear us down and discourage us so we'll quit. Our Father often requires us to persevere while we wait for manifestation of the answers to our prayers.

Sometimes we're required to persevere in faith for several months and sometimes for many years. *We must understand that God's delay is not necessarily a denial.*

All Christians should pray continually. If we fail to pray continually, we disobey the instructions in the Word of God. When we disobey our Father's instructions, we *sin* against Him. "*...far be it from me that I should sin against the Lord by ceasing to pray for you...*" (I Samuel 12:23).

All Christians know the Lord's Prayer. Let's look at what God's Word says immediately before and after the familiar words of this prayer. Jesus was asked by His disciples how they should pray. "Then He was praying in a certain place; and when He stopped, one of His disciples said to Him, Lord, teach us to pray, [just] as John taught his disciples" (Luke 11:1).

Jesus answered with the following words which we call the Lord's Prayer. "And He said to them, When you pray, say: Our Father Who is in heaven, hallowed be Your name, Your kingdom come. Your will be done [held holy and revered] on earth as it is in heaven. Give us daily our bread [food for the morrow]. And forgive us our sins, for we ourselves also forgive everyone who is indebted to us [who has offended us or done us wrong]. And bring us not into temptation but rescue us from evil" (Luke 11:2-4).

These are wonderful words, *but we must not stop here. Do you know* what Jesus said in the passages of Scripture immediately following these words? "And He said to them, Which of you who has a friend will go to him at midnight and will say to him, Friend, lend me three loaves [of bread], for a friend of mine who is on a journey has just come, and I have nothing to put before him; and he from within will answer, Do not disturb me; the door is now closed, and my children are with me in bed; I cannot get up and supply you [with anything]? I tell you, *although he will not get up and supply him anything because he is his friend, yet because of his shameless persistence and insistence he will get up and give him as much as he needs"* (Luke 11:5-8).

In this parable, Jesus spoke of a man who visited his friend at midnight asking him to lend him three loaves of bread. His sleepy friend thought this request was unreasonable. He told his friend that he didn't want to be disturbed because he had retired for the night.

However, the friend *refused to be denied.* He wouldn't go away. He kept asking the man for three loaves of bread. He continued to knock on his door. *Friendship wasn't enough to get the other man up, but perseverance caused him to arise.* He gave the other man three loaves of bread because of his persistence.

Jesus explained this parable with the following statement. *"So I say to you, Ask and keep on asking and it shall be given you; seek and keep on seeking and you shall find; knock and keep on knocking and the door shall be opened to you. For everyone who asks and keeps on asking receives; and he who seeks and keeps on seeking finds; and to him who knocks and keeps on knocking, the door shall be opened"* (Luke 11:9-10).

Whenever anything is repeated in the Bible, this repetition is done for purposes of emphasis. Please go back and underline or highlight the number of times the words *keep on* or *keeps on* are used in this passage of Scripture. Jesus used these words *six times. He wants us to persevere when we pray. We must not give up!*

Shortly after this, Jesus told another parable to further illustrate the importance of perseverance in prayer. This parable is quite long. Let's look at it in three parts. "Also

[Jesus] told them a parable to the effect that they ought *always to pray and not to turn coward (faint, lose heart, and give up)*. He said, In a certain city there was a judge who neither reverenced and feared God nor respected or considered man. And there was a widow in that city who *kept coming to him* and saying, Protect and defend and give me justice against my adversary" (Luke 18:1-3).

This parable starts by telling us we should never give up when we pray. Jesus told the apostles about a judge who wasn't influenced by reverence for God or consideration for other human beings. He told of a widow who *kept coming* to this judge for justice.

Was the widow's perseverance effective? "And for a time he would not; but later he said to himself, Though I have neither reverence or fear for God not respect or consideration for man, *yet because this widow continues to bother me*, I will defend and protect and avenge her, lest she give me intolerable annoyance and *wear me out by her continual coming* or at the last she come and rail on me or assault me or strangle me" (Luke 18:4-5).

Even though the judge initially refused to answer the widow's request, he finally decided that, although he had no reverence for God or man, he would answer this request *because of her perseverance*. The widow refused to be denied. Her perseverance was *the only reason* the judge gave in.

Jesus then closed this parable by *telling us to persevere in our prayers* just as this widow persevered with the judge. "Then the Lord said, Listen to what the unjust judge says! And will not [our just] God defend and protect and avenge His elect (His chosen ones), *who cry to Him day and night*? Will He defer them and delay help on their behalf? I tell you, He will defend and protect and avenge them speedily. *However, when the Son of Man comes, will He find [persistence in] faith on the earth?"* (Luke 18:6-8).

Jesus compared the unjust judge to just God. If this unjust judge would respond because of perseverance, *will not our Father respond even more when we persevere in our prayers?* We should cry out to God day and night. We live in the last days before Jesus returns. *We must add perseverance to our faith when we pray.*

This chapter is filled with instructions encouraging us to persevere in prayer. In the next chapter, we'll look into God's Word to see *why* our Father often requires us to wait to receive the manifestation of His answer to our prayers.

Chapter 18

Why Do We Have to Wait?

Most of us want an *immediate* answer to prayer. We want our answer from God and it we want it *now*. We're like the Psalmist David who said, "Answer me *speedily*, O Lord, for my spirit fails..." (Psalm 143:7).

Many people can't understand why they have to go through long, drawn out ordeals. Our Father knows exactly what the future holds. If we have to go through a prolonged period of adversity to prepare us for the future, our Father knows this season of adversity actually can turn into a blessing.

When we go through difficult times, we should try to see this season of adversity from our Father's perspective. "...My son, do not think lightly or scorn to submit to the correction and discipline of the Lord, *nor lose courage and give up and faint* when you are reproved or corrected by Him; for the Lord corrects and disciplines *everyone* whom He loves, and He punishes, even scourges, *every* son whom He accepts and welcomes to His heart and cherishes" (Hebrews 12:5-6).

Those of us who are parents often have to discipline our children to help them grow and mature. Our heavenly Father is no different. We *must not give up* when our Father allows us to go through a season of adversity for purposes of correction. Our Father allows these things to happen *because He loves us.*

The carnal part of us would like to live easy lives without problems. Our Father doesn't look at our lives from this perspective. His Word actually instructs us to *rejoice* when we go through difficult times."...*[let us also be full of joy now!] let us exult and triumph in our troubles and rejoice in our sufferings, knowing that pressure and affliction and hardship produce patient and unswerving endurance. And endurance (fortitude) develops maturity of character (approved faith and tried integrity). And character (of this sort) produces [the habit of] joyful and confident hope of eternal salvation"* (Romans 5:3-4).

Let's examine the last part of this passage of Scripture first because this portion tells us the benefits our Father wants us to receive. Would you like to have *maturity of character*? Would you like to have a *strong faith* that is *proven and dependable*? Would you like to *maintain your integrity at all times*? Most people would answer "Yes" to each of these questions.

Now let's examine the first portion of this passage of Scripture. Our Father says we should be *filled with joy* when we are faced with trouble. He instructs us to *exult* in our troubles. We should leap for joy. Our Father actually wants us to be *jubilant* when we go through difficult times. He wants us to be *glad* when we're suffering. *God's ways certainly are different from our ways, aren't they?*

Our Father wants us to rejoice because He wants us to understand that pressure, affliction and hardship are able to produce desirable character traits in us. If we react to adversity the way God's Word instructs us to react, *we will become more patient and enduring. Our faith will grow. We will be honest at all times.*

If we really trust our Father, we'll obey the instructions in His Word. Even though it may seem strange to our carnal nature, God really does want us to rejoice when we go through adversity. *"Consider it wholly joyful, my brethren, whenever you are enveloped in or encounter trials of any sort or fall into various temptations. Be assured and understand that the trial and proving of your faith bring out endurance and steadfastness and patience. But let endurance and steadfastness and patience have full play and do a thorough work, so that you may be [people] perfectly and fully developed [with no defects], lacking in nothing"* (James 1:2-4).

Once again, let's look at the last portion of the passage of Scripture first because this portion tells us the benefits we will receive. Would you like to be *perfectly and fully developed*? Would you like to be a person with *no defects*? Would you like your Father to look at you and say that you *lack nothing*? Would you like to be *more patient, enduring* and *steadfast* than you are now? Would you like your *faith* to be *proven* and *reliable*?

I believe you will answer "Yes" to each of these questions. There is *only one way* to develop these very desirable character traits. *We must go through trials and tribulations and react to them according to the instructions in the Word of God.* We should rejoice because of the magnificent opportunities the trials in our lives provide for us. *"Happy* and *fortunate* is the man whom God reproves; so do *not* despise or reject the correction of the Almighty [subjecting you to *trial* and *suffering*]" (Job 5:17).

Many middle-aged and older people have come to realize the things that seemed to be the worst things that ever happened to them often have turned into blessings. Sometimes our Father has to allow us to go through a difficult and prolonged season in our lives so He can mold us and shape us. Although it's difficult to believe when we're in the midst of these problems, we actually are blessed to be corrected by God.

We must trust our Father. Whenever we go through a difficult season of adversity, I believe we should say something like this. "Dear Father, I rejoice because of this *opportunity* to mature and develop my character. In the name of Jesus Christ, I ask You to show me *exactly what You want me to learn* as I go through this affliction. Please help me to make the necessary changes so I can arrive safely on the other side to become exactly what You want me to become."

Our Father won't allow us to go through something we can't bear. He always provides us with a way of escape. "...*no temptation* (no trial regarded as enticing to sin, no matter how it comes or where it leads) has overtaken you and laid hold on you that is not *common to man* [that is, no temptation or trial has come to you that is beyond human resistance and that is not adjusted and adapted and belonging to human experience, and such as man can bear]. But *God is faithful* [to His Word and to His compassionate nature], and *He [can be trusted] not to let you be tempted and tried and assayed beyond your ability and strength of resistance and power to endure,* but with the temptation He will *[always]* also provide the *way out* (the means of *escape* to a landing place), that you may be capable and strong and powerful to bear up under it *patiently*" (I Corinthians 10:13).

These words are encouraging! Sometimes it seems as if we're faced with problems that are greater than we can endure, but God's Word says this isn't so. Our Father is faithful and compassionate. We can trust Him completely. He will *never* allow us to go through more than we can endure.

This passage of Scripture goes on to say that our Father will *always* provide us with a way out. We can bear up patiently under our problems if we *know* our Father will never allow us to face more than we can bear and if we *know* He will always provide the means of escape. Whenever we face a difficult and enduring problem that doesn't seem to have a solution, I believe we should meditate constantly on the promises in this passage of Scripture.

If we truly seek to carry out God's will for our lives, we must endure patiently. *"Do not, therefore, fling away* your *fearless confidence,* for it carries a great and glorious compensation of reward. For you have need of *steadfast patience and endurance,* so that you may perform and fully accomplish the *will of God,* and thus receive and carry away [and enjoy to the full] what is promised"* (Hebrews 10:35-36).

We must not throw away our confidence. Our Father wants us to endure. We can't carry out His will for our lives if we give up. Great rewards await God's children who persevere with faith to carry out their Father's will for their lives. We will enjoy rewards here on earth as a result of the inner fulfillment we will experience from being in the center of God's will. We also will receive wonderful eternal rewards at the judgment seat of Christ. Our Father promises to provide us with *great and glorious compensation.*

We must trust our Father. *If* we love Him, and *if* we strongly desire to carry out His will, we can be assured that He will cause *everything* to work together for good. *"We are assured and know that [God being a partner in their labor] all things work together and are [fitting into a plan] for good to and for those who love God and are called according to [His] design and purpose"* (Romans 8:28).

This passage of Scripture often is misunderstood. It doesn't merely say that all things work together for good. There are *conditions* to this promise. All things work together for good *if* we love God and *if* we are called according to His design and purpose for our lives.

If we love God, we will *obey* His instructions. If we do our best to obey the instructions in God's Word, to follow the leading of the Holy Spirit and to wholeheartedly seek His will for our lives, He then promises that all things will work together for good. *We can trust our Father to honor this promise.*

The apostle Paul was a mature man of God. He experienced a great deal of adversity in his life. However, he learned to accept these problems and remain contented. Paul said, *"...I have learned how to be content (satisfied to the point where I am not disturbed or disquieted) in whatever state I am"* (Philippians 4:11).

The Lord will bless us if we learn to remain calm in the midst of adversity. *"Blessed (happy, fortunate, to be envied) is the man whom You discipline and instruct, O Lord, and teach out of Your law that You may give him power to keep himself calm in the days of adversity..."* (Psalm 94:12-13).

We don't have enough human power to stay calm in the midst of severe adversity. This passage of Scripture says that God gives us this power when He disciplines us and we learn from Him.

Our Father doesn't want us to allow the problems of life to disturb us. If we really believe He is in complete control of everything, why would we be disturbed? If we really believe our Father is able to cause everything to work together for good, we will be able to remain calm at all times. We will be able to rejoice when we go through a season of adversity.

We must know and trust the promises in God's Word. Satan wants us to be *impatient pessimists*. Our Father wants us to be *patient optimists*. Our Father promises to provide wonderful blessings to every one of His children who seek His will wholeheartedly and refuse to give up.

We *don't* develop character and maturity on the *mountain tops* of life. These desirable qualities are developed in the *valleys*. We can only grow and mature spiritually if we trust our Father completely and persevere continually as we seek to carry out His plan for our lives.

Conclusion

This book contains *almost three hundred Scripture references* to help you increase your patience and perseverance. When it doesn't seem as if you can go one step farther, these instructions can help you to persevere to carry out your Father's will for your life.

Please don't make the mistake of reading this book only one time. The Scripture references contained in this book will only help you if you're able to get them up off the printed page, into your *mind* and then down into your *heart*. We get Scripture into our *minds* by *studying* God's Word. Scripture drops from our minds down into our *hearts* when we continually *meditate* on it.

This is a book to *study*, not just a book to read. I urge you to take the test on the following pages to see how much you have absorbed. I believe you'll find that additional study and meditation are required to appropriate the instructions from God's Word that are explained in this book.

Once you have finished the following test, please go back through the book and study and meditate on the areas where additional knowledge is required. Persevere until you believe you have a full understanding of every passage of Scripture in this book. Then, set the book aside for at least thirty days.

After this period of time has elapsed, take the test again. See for yourself how much information about patience, endurance and perseverance you have been able to *retain*. Tests have shown that a high percentage of what we learn disappears completely from our consciousness within thirty days. *Repetition* is extremely important to spiritual growth.

I pray that this book will be a great blessing to you. I hope you'll share *Never, Never Give Up* with others. Thank you and God bless you.

What Did You Learn
From This Book?

Question	Page Reference
1. How would you describe someone who is a patient person?	10
2. How would you describe a persevering person?	11
3. What quality does the Bible say must be added to our faith to inherit the promises of God?	14
4. Our Father wants His children to be steadfast. What does it mean to be "steadfast?"	15
5. How does *The Amplified Bible* define patience?	15
6. What quality does the Word of God say we should develop in order to develop steadfastness?	16
7. If we hope for something that is unseen, what two qualities are required to be present while we wait for what we hope for to be manifested?	16
8. What three areas of our personality constitute our souls?	16
9. What qualities did Jesus say were necessary for us to control our souls?	16
10. Why do pride and impatience go together?	16-17
11. Why do humility and patience go together?	17
12. Many of us hang on to our problems instead of giving them to God. How exactly does the Bible tell us to release our anxieties, worries and concerns to God?	17
13. Many of us give our problems to God and then take them back when it doesn't seem as if we will get an answer. *The Amplified Bible* uses four words to tell us how many times we should give our problems to our Father. What are these four words?	17
14. What does the Bible refer to when it speaks of casting bread upon water and how does this relate to our need for patience?	18

15. The Word of God compares our need for patience with the patience exhibited by farmers. What comparison would you give between your need for patience and the farmer who had planted a crop? 18-19

16. Give examples of the driving habits of many people and the relationship of these driving habits upon their patience? 20-22

17. Is there a relationship between rapidly prepared food and our patience? 22

18. Give examples of several things that most people do today that have an effect upon their level of patience. 22-24

19. Is there a relationship between high school dropouts, job hopping and changing churches and our patience? 24-25

20. What does the Bible say about "get rich quick" schemes? How does this desire affect our patience? 25-26

21. What diversions do lonely and impatient people often rely upon to help them overcome being alone? 26

22. How would you describe the relationship between athletic teams and the overall patience among people today? 26-27

23. What relationship is there between financial debts and impatience? 27

24. Why is God so patient with the sin in the world today? 29

25. Jesus Christ made a statement at the age of twelve that gives us a clear indication of His great patience. What did Jesus say and how did this statement indicate that He was extremely patient before the start of His earthly ministry? 30-31

26. Jesus exhibited great patience with Saul of Tarsus who spent many years persecuting Christians. After the miracle which changed Saul's name to Paul,

50. Instead of hurrying, what specific instructions does the Word of God give us?   48

51. How do we know exactly when the sun rises and sets each day and when the seasons of the moon will change each month? How should this knowledge encourage us when we're waiting for God to answer our prayers?   48-49

52. When Jesus heard that Lazarus was sick, did He immediately rush to the side of Lazarus?

53. What did Jesus find when He arrived at Bethany where Lazarus was?   49-50

54. Martha knew her brother would not have died if Jesus had arrived in time. Did she complain about the delay?   50

55. How did Jesus respond to Martha?   50

56. When we wait for God to answer our prayers, why is it important for us to turn away from the fast pace of the world we live in?   51

57. What specific advice did Jesus give us in regard to concerning ourselves about the future?   52

58. When Jesus asked His Father to provide our bread, what period of time did He ask God to provide for?   52

59. For what period of time has God promised to provide the strength, rest and security we need?   52

60. Instead of being concerned with external events, why is it important for us to live from the inside out when we're faced with severe pressure?   52-53

61. What specific advice does Psalm 46:10 give us that will quiet and calm us when we're faced with severe pressure?   53

62. How does God look at our actions when we hurry and rush ahead of Him?   53-54

63. What specifically does the Bible tell us will happen to everyone who is impatient and hasty?   54

196. The Word of God gives us a conditional promise telling us that God will listen to all of our prayers. What is the one condition for Him to do this?   131

197. The next verse of Scripture continues this conditional promise. If we meet the condition mentioned in the previous verse of Scripture, how many prayers can we expect God to answer? When does God answer?   132

198. Jesus promised us that we would receive whatever we ask for in prayer. However, there was a condition to this statement Jesus made. What was this condition?   132

199. On another occasion, Jesus told us to ask whatever we want in prayer and He said it would be done for us. However, there were two conditions to this promise. What were these conditions?   132-133

200. The Word of God says that a certain type of prayer makes the tremendous, dynamic power of God available to us. What type of prayer brings this spiritual power into manifestation?   133

201. When we pray continually for members of our family to become Christians and they show no sign whatsoever of becoming Christians, what should we do?   133-135

202. Almost all Christians know the Lord's prayer. However, do you know what important lesson Jesus taught in a parable immediately following the Lord's prayer?   135-136

203. When Jesus explained the meaning of this parable, He used two words six different times. What are these two words and why did Jesus place so much emphasis on them?   136

204. Shortly after this, Jesus told another parable. He told about a widow who went before a judge with a specific request. The judge eventually

granted her request. What was the reason why he
granted her request? 36-137

05. How did Jesus compare this unjust judge to God?
What lesson was Jesus trying to teach in this
parable? 137-138

206. Sometimes our Father has to correct and discipline
us just as those of us who are parents often have to
discipline and correct our children. What specific
advice does God's Word give us when we are
corrected by God? 139

207. Our Father tells us to be filled with joy and to exult
when we go through troubles and to rejoice in our
suffering. Why does He tell us to do this? 140

208. God's Word says we can be perfectly and fully
developed and that we will lack nothing. It says
that we can increase our patience and our faith.
How do we achieve these desirable results? 141

209. Sometimes it seems as if our problems are more
than we can endure. What does the Word of God
say about this? 142-143

210. Why does the Word of God tell us not to throw
away our confidence? What does God promise
for His children who refuse to do this because
they have steadfast patience and endurance? 143

211. Romans 8:28 is a familiar verse of Scripture.
Most Christians know that it says that all things
work together for good. However, there are two
conditions to this promise. What are these
conditions? 143-144

212. What desirable state did the apostle Paul say he
had learned to achieve no matter problems he
was faced with? 144

213. Psalm 94:12-13 tells us a specific reason why God
discipline, instructs and teaches us. Why does our
Father do this? 144-145

67

Appendix

Have You Entered Into the Kingdom of God?

You have just a read a complete set of instructions telling us how to increase our patience and perseverance. These instructions are given to God's children — those human beings who have entered into His kingdom. I ask each reader of this book, *"Have you entered into the Kingdom of God?"*

We *don't* enter into the kingdom of God by church attendance, baptism, confirmation, teaching Sunday school or living a good life. Jesus Christ paid the price for each and every one of us to enter this kingdom. He said, *"...I assure you, most solemnly I tell you, that unless a person is born again (anew, from above), he cannot ever see (know, be acquainted with, and experience) the kingdom of God"* (John 3:3).

Some people are so caught up with their own religious denomination or their personal beliefs that they completely miss God's instructions on how to enter His kingdom. We must be reborn spiritually! This starts by *admitting* that we're sinners. Then we must *repent* of these sins. *"...unless you repent (change your mind for the better and heartily amend your ways, with abhorrence of your past sins) you will all likewise perish and be lost eternally"* (Luke 13:5).

Many people miss out on eternal life in heaven because they are trusting in the goodness of their own lives to get them to heaven. This is a tragic mistake! *With the exception of Jesus Christ, every person who has ever lived has been a sinner. "...None is righteous, just and truthful and upright and conscientious, no, not one"* (Romans 3:10).

We are *all* sinners! *"...all have sinned and are falling short of the honor and glory which god bestows and receives"* (Romans 3:23) God *doesn't* have degrees of sin. If we have committed *one* sin, we're *just as guilty* as someone who has committed many sins! *"For whosoever keeps the Law [as a] whole but stumbles and offends in one [single instance] has become guilty of [breaking] all of it"* (James 2:10).

In addition to acknowledging our sins and repenting of them, there is *one additional step* we must take. *"...if you acknowledge and confess with your lips that Jesus is Lord and in your heart believe (adhere to, trust in and rely on the truth) that God raised Him from the dead, you will be saved. For with the heart a person believes (adheres to, trusts in, and relies on Christ) and so is justified (declared righteous, acceptable to God), and with the mouth confesses (declares openly and speaks out freely his faith) and confirms [his] salvation"* (Romans 10:9-10).

We must do more than pay mental assent to trust Jesus for eternal salvation. *We also must believe this deep in our hearts.* All of our hope for eternal life in heaven must be based on deep faith that Jesus paid the price for our sins.

If we really believe this truth in our hearts, we'll open our mouths and tell others. We should tell other people that we're Christians and that we trust completely in Jesus Christ for our eternal salvation. We aren't saved until we believe this in our hearts and confess it with our mouths!

All of us were born naturally on the day our mothers gave birth. In order to be reborn spiritually, we must have a *second* birth. *"You have been regenerated (born again), not from a mortal origin (seed, sperm), but from one that is immortal by the ever living and lasting Word of God"* (I Peter 1:23).

God wants us to come to Him as *little children*. He doesn't reveal Himself to us through our *intellects*. He reveals Himself through our *hearts*. We may be adults in the natural world, but we need to start all over again in the spiritual realm. We must have *childlike faith*. *"...unless you repent (change, turn about) and become like little children [trusting, lowly, loving, forgiving], you can never enter the kingdom of heaven [at all]"* (Matthew 18:3).

The following prayer will result in your spiritual rebirth if you truly believe these truths in your heart and also tell others what you believe:

"Father God, I come to you in the name of Jesus Christ. I admit I am a sinner. I know there is no way I can enter into Your kingdom based upon the sinful life I've led. I'm genuinely sorry for my sins and I ask for Your mercy. I believe in my heart that Jesus Christ is Your Son. I believe He was born of a virgin and that He died on the cross to pay for my sins. I believe You raised Him from the dead and He is alive today. I trust completely in Him as my only way of entering Your kingdom. Thank You, Father. Amen."

If you pray this prayer from your heart, and tell this exciting news to other people, *you have been reborn spiritually*. You have a fresh, new start. *"...if any person is [ingrafted] in Christ (the Messiah) he is a new creation (a new creature altogether); the old [previous moral and spiritual condition] has passed away. Behold, the fresh and new has come!"* (I Corinthians 5:17).

Welcome into the family of God!

We Offer You a Substantial Quantity Discount

Has this book helped you? Would you like to share it with other Christians who need to know the truth about perseverance and endurance? Perhaps even more important, would you share the facts in this book with people who are not Christians?

In order to encourage readers to share this and other books and cassette tapes by Jack Hartman, we offer you a **40% quantity discount** when you order five to nine books or cassette tapes. We offer you a **50% discount** on order of ten or more books or cassette tapes.

For example, if you order ten copies of this book, you can share this with others for only **$3.98 per copy** plus the shipping and handling charge.

In the back of this book we have detailed information on all books and cassette tapes by Jack Hartman. Take advantage of our liberal discount policy to order many of these books and tapes for your own use or to give others.

A Request to Our Readers

If this book has helped you, *we would like your comments so we can share them with others.* We want to tell the facts about persevering and enduring in the face of adversity to many people. *Your comments can help to convince them of the importance of carefully studying the information contained in this book.*

When we receive a letter containing comments on any of my books or cassette tapes, we prayerfully take out excerpts from these letters. Selected excerpts are then included in our advertising and promotional material.

If this book has been a blessing to you, please write to me in care of the publisher. Tell me in your own words what this book has meant to you and why you would recommend it to others. Please give as *much* information as you can.

Also, we will need your *written permission* to use all or any part of your comments. We will never list your name or street address. We simply use the initials of your first and last name and the state or country you live in. (Example — G.G., Illinois).

Thank you for taking a few minutes to help us and, even more important, to help others.

Jack Hartman
Lamplight Ministries
Box 1307
Dunedin, FL 34697

Trust God For Your Finances

Trust God For Your Finances is Jack Hartman's best-selling book. Even though he was a completely unknown author when he wrote it, this book now has almost 120,000 copies in print. It has been translated into several foreign languages.

Many readers approach books on this vital subject with skepticism and caution because they're afraid it's another "get rich quick" book. Readers will quickly find that this book is filled with realistic ways to put the Lord first in every area of our lives.

It compares prosperity from God's point of view with the world's system of prosperity. This book contains exhaustive Scripture references. It's saturated with the Word of God.

This practical book is written in simple, straightforward, easy-to-read style. It's balanced, comprehensive, and informative. It contains many concepts that aren't contained in similar books on this subject.

Jack Hartman believes we're on the verge of a world-wide economic recession. However, he teaches that God's principles of prosperity aren't in any way dependent upon worldly conditions.

We're convinced that this book will help any reader who is interested in this important subject. You have no risk in ordering it. We offer it, as well as all of our other products, with an unconditional money-back guarantee. Our quantity discount provision enables you to purchase copies of this book for as little as **$3.48 a copy.**

What Will Heaven Be Like?

Recent polls indicate that approximately 75 percent of the American people believe in heaven. However, even many people who are Christians know very little about heaven. Jack Hartman has spent hundreds of hours searching the Scriptures to write this book, *What Will Heaven Be Like?* This book is solidly anchored in the Word of God, containing 214 Scripture references.

This book explains that we'll experience great exhilaration when angels carry us to heaven immediately after we die. It describes from the holy Scriptures what it will be like to see the glory of God with our own eyes. We'll experience a wonderful reunion with our Christian loved ones who died and went to heaven before us. They'll be in perfect health and happier than we've ever seen them.

Jack searched the Word of God to explain why self-centeredness will not exist in heaven. There are no walls between people in heaven. Everyone there will be unselfish, humble and loving.

The holy city of New Jerusalem is described in detail. Jack explains from the Word of God the breathtaking panorama of mountains, hills, foothills and sparkling, crystal-clear rivers that we'll see in heaven. Beautiful heavenly orchards will produce twelve magnificent varieties of fruit.

This book explains in detail many facts about our wonderful new heavenly bodies and the rewards that Christians will receive at the Judgment Seat of Christ. It explains the joy and eternal fulfillment that will be available to all Christians in heaven.

What Will Heaven Be Like? is also an effective evangelistic tool. Two chapters near the end of the book clearly explain what salvation is ... why we must be saved ... how we become saved ... where we'll live eternally if Jesus is our Savior ... and where we'll live eternally if He isn't.

We want to make it as easy as possible for you to distribute this message. Because of this, our quantity discount method of purchasing books will make this book available to you for a price as low as **$3.48 per copy.**

Strong Faith For the Last Days

In recent years, many people have experienced severe problems. Are these problems part of the last days before Jesus Christ returns? Whether they are or not, many people would like to know exactly how to develop a stronger faith to enable them to trust the Lord to help them with the difficult problems they face.

In this book, Jack Hartman explains exactly how to strengthen our faith. Over 300 Scripture references are used to show Christians exactly how to increase their faith in the living God.

Seventeen Scripture references are used to explain how to pray according to our Father's will and how to receive answers to our prayers. Christians will learn how much faith they were given when they became Christians and how to increase this faith.

Strong faith can only be developed upon a solid foundation. An entire chapter is devoted to explaining what this foundation is and how to build our faith upon it.

Readers will learn an effective method of studying the Bible in order to increase their faith. Two chapters are devoted to Christian meditation. What does it mean to "meditate day and night" on the Word of God? How do we do this?

This exciting book contains over 200 pages that are filled with specific instructions telling us how to increase our faith. It's written in a clear and easy to understand style. Every principle that is explained is thoroughly documented by several Scripture references.

Life is becoming more difficult, and we need specific instructions on how to deal with adversity. We believe this book will help many people to deal with the problems we all face. In our efforts to share our books with as many people as possible, our quantity discount system will make this book available to you for a price of **only $3.98.**

Deep Inner Peace

Deep Inner Peace is Jack Hartman's second bestselling book. It's filled with specific principles telling the reader how to enter into God's rest, overcome worry and to develop quiet trust in the Lord. We believe this book will help many readers to develop a calm assurance that the Lord is in complete control of every area of our lives.

Three readers have told us they were on the verge of suicide when they read this book. Other people have written to say they have been helped with drug and alcohol problems. We believe this book will help many readers to become much more calm and relaxed.

Several people have written to us commenting on the peace that came over them as they studied and meditated on the Scriptural contents of this book. *Deep Inner Peace* is the result of exhaustive research and study in the Word of God. It contains over 200 Scripture references.

The practical principles in this valuable book will open a whole new world for many readers. Our quantity discount provision enables you to purchase one copy of this book for as little as **$3.48 a copy**. As always, our unconditional money-back guarantee applies.

Conquering Fear

Jack Hartman believes fear will increase significantly in the world in the years immediately ahead of us. Many people who are now secure in various forms of worldly security will be consumed by fear when this security is taken away from them.

Our heavenly Father doesn't want His children to be afraid. He tells us 366 times in His Word that He doesn't want us to be afraid. He tells us once for every day in the year and once for leap year. If God repeats something 366 times, He obviously must mean it.

Jesus Christ has delivered us from fear. He has given us victory over fear. Jack Hartman knows what it is to be paralyzed by fear. He has spent hundred of hours studying the Word of God to learn everything it teaches about overcoming fear.

II Timothy 1:7 speaks of the "spirit of fear." Much of the fear in our lives comes from a spiritual source — Satan. Christians must not give in to the spirit of fear. This book gives many specific examples of how the spirit of fear tries to get at us and it gives many specific techniques from the Bible to overcome this.

It explains the definite relationship between pride and fear and why humility and love are so vitally important in overcoming fear. The Word of God teaches us that perfect love is the key to overcoming fear.

What is perfect love? How do we become perfected in love? Several chapters are devoted to answering these specific questions.

The book closes with a chapter titled "Fear and the Aging Process." As we grow older, many of us become more vulnerable because of the problems of aging. Jack Hartman gives many specific examples of the way fear attacks older people and he explains how to overcome this.

We believe this book will be very valuable to you and also to other people you know. With our quantity discount program, you can receive a copy of this book for only **$3.48 a copy.**

God's Will For Our Lives

GOD'S WILL FOR OUR LIVES

HOW TO FIND IT, ENTER INTO IT, AND REMAIN IN IT

JACK HARTMAN

In *God's Will For Our Lives*, Jack Hartman examines questions that many thinking people ask ... Why are we here? ... What does God want us to do with our lives? ... How can we find meaning, purpose and fulfillment in our lives?

Before we were formed in our mother's womb, God had a definite plan for each of our lives. He gave each of us special abilities to carry out the assignment He has for us.

We must not waste our lives doing what we want to do. God's will for our lives is beautiful. Our personal goals are ugly when we look at them from God's point of view.

Many Christians are caught up doing what they think is important. We must learn to turn away from our own desires and seek our Father's will for our lives with all our hearts.

He gave us His Word to provide general directions for all of His children. He gave us the Holy Spirit to provide us with specific guidance every step of the way. Unfortunately, many Christians are unable to hear the still, small voice of the Holy Spirit.

We all crave fulfillment. No one wants to live an empty life. Unfortunately, as many of us grow older, we find the things that once satisfied do not satisfy any longer. Only God's will for our lives can provide true and lasting satisfaction.

It isn't too late for Christians to find God's will for their lives. We must not feel guilty if we haven't yet found what our Creator called us to do. In this book, Jack Hartman has written on a difficult subject in a clear and easy to understand style.

We believe this book will open new horizons and help many readers to find God's will for their lives. With our quantity discount program, you can receive a copy of this book for only **$3.48 a copy.**

Soaring Above the Problems of Life

Soaring Above the Problems of Life is a book that will be an immense help to anyone who is going through severe trials. This book really isn't meaningful to people who find everything going well in their lives. However, it's a lifesaver to people who are faced with severe adversity.

This practical, "hands-on" book is filled with facts from the Word of God. This book isn't theoretical in any way. Jack Hartman has applied these principles in his own life and we have received many letters from readers who have been helped by the Scriptural principles in this book.

Sometimes our heavenly Father has to allow severe problems to come into our lives because He knows this is the only way we'll grow and mature. We all would like to have more character and maturity, but the truth is that everyone with a lot of character and maturity has been through trials and tribulations.

Many times the adversities in our lives are actually our greatest blessings. The important thing in life isn't what happens to us. Christians need to learn to react the way God's Word says we should react.

Many of us allow our problems to seem much bigger than they really are and God to seem much smaller than He really is. Man's impossibilities are God's opportunities.

When we're faced with problems we can't solve, we know the One Who knows how to solve them. His ways are vastly different from ours. We must learn His ways instead of trying to do everything with our own ability.

God's strength is made perfect in our weakness. When we admit our helplessness, this often opens the door to His help. Study this book which is filled with hundreds of Scripture references to see exactly what the Word of God has to say about how to deal with the severe problems of life.

In an effort to make this book available to everyone we possibly can, we make possible the purchase of this book for only **$3.48 a copy** when purchased as part of our top quantity discount. We pray that this book will bless you.

How to Study the Bible

Jack Hartman has taught almost 800 Bible study classes. He has found that many Christians try to study the Bible and give up because they're unable to find a fruitful method of Bible study. *How to Study the Bible* explains the method Jack uses to study the Bible.

This is a practical, step-by-step method of studying God's Word. This logical, sensible method of Bible study is clear, concise and easy to understand. It will help Christians to get the Word of God up off the printed page and into their minds and hearts.

Jack Hartman believes it is vitally important for Christians to learn the importance of studying the Bible instead of just reading it. Many people have written to say that this proven, effective method of Bible study has given them a spiritual breakthrough and added a new dimension to their lives.

There are no shortcuts to this system. Hard work and discipline are required. We know anyone who pays the price of doing this will find the rewards are well worth the effort.

In our efforts to share our books with as many people as possible, our quantity discount system will make this book available to you for a price of **only $2.50.**

100 Years From Today

In 1975, Jack Hartman started a Bible study class in the insurance office he operated. Within one year, this grew to the point where 300 to 350 people were attending the class each Tuesday night.

In those early days, Jack produced a mimeographed Bible study on the importance of salvation. Many students from his class reported that this mimeographed Bible study had been used effectively to win people to Christ. As a result, this early Bible study was rewritten in book form with the title *100 Years From Today.*

This book is written in a clear, conversational style. It explains what salvation is, why we must be saved, how to become saved and where we'll be one hundred years from now if we are saved — and if we are not.

This book clearly explains the message of salvation through Jesus Christ. It closes by asking the reader to make a decision and to make it now. It explains that this is the most important decision any of us will ever make.

This book is simple and to the point. The reader won't be confused by complex theological language. We believe you'll find this book to be an excellent tool to win unbelievers to Christ.

We're all called to share the gospel of Jesus Christ. Many Christians don't know how to do this. We believe you'll find this book to be extremely valuable to help your friends, acquaintances and loved ones understand the absolute necessity of asking Jesus Christ to come into their lives.

We want to make it as easy as possible for you to distribute this message. Because of this, our quantity discount method of purchasing books will make this book available to you for a price as low as **$2.00 per copy.**

Nuggets of Faith

Jack Hartman

As soon as Jack Hartman became a Christian, he started to write spiritual meditations virtually every day. Jack has now written more than 100,000 of these meditations. The book, *Nuggets of Faith*, shares his best meditations on the subject of faith.

This book contains 78 "nuggets." Each "nugget" (average length is 3 paragraphs) is the result of many hours of research and study.

There are no wasted words in this book. Each "nugget" goes straight to the point. We believe these short, capsulized thoughts will give many readers fresh spiritual insight.

This book is clear and easy to understand. It is very practical and helpful. It will give you maximum results in a minimum amount of time.

Many readers can easily read this book in one day. On the other hand, many of these "nuggets" contain enough spiritual depth so you can take one "nugget" with you in the morning and dwell on it throughout the day, turning its Scriptural truth over and over in your mind as you meditate on how this truth can apply to your life.

We have a sincere desire to enable you to share as many of these books as possible with others. Because of this, our quantity discount program will make it possible for you to purchase copies of *Nuggets of Faith* for as little as **$2.00 per copy.**

Increased Energy and Vitality

Jack and Judy Hartman are determined to be in the best possible condition to serve Jesus Christ during the reminder of their lives. Because of this common goal, they have spent hundreds of hours of study and practical trial and error to find the best way to increase their energy and vitality. This book is solidly based upon more than two hundred Scripture references.

Jack and Judy explain in detail the simple, inexpensive and enjoyable exercise program they follow. Several chapters are devoted to a scriptural explanation of the energizing power of the Word of God and what the Bible says about utilizing the unlimited energy of the Holy Spirit.

Increased Energy and Vitality carefully examines what the holy Scriptures say about the food our Father has provided to give us fuel to produce maximum energy and vitality. It also gives a thorough scriptural explanation of why people overeat, how to stop overeating and how to take off weight and keep it off.

Studies have shown that the digestion of food requires more energy than any other bodily function. This book carefully examines the problems that over one hundred million Americans experience in this area. It gives practical solutions to these problems.

The authors explain why they believe vitamin and mineral supplements and free-form amino acids are important. Most of us lubricate our automobiles regularly and fail to lubricate our bodies. We believe you'll be interested to learn what our Creator wants us to do to lubricate our bodies.

Approximately one out of every three Americans has problems sleeping. Many scriptural instructions are combined with practical suggestions to increase energy and vitality through improved sleep with the use of sleeping pills. The book concludes with several of Judy Hartman's fat-free, sugar-free recipes for tasty meals that will provide maximum energy and vitality.

We have a sincere desire to share as many of these books as possible with others. Because of this, our quantity discount program will make it possible for you to purchase copies of *Increased Energy and Vitality* for as little as **$4.98 per copy.**

Cassette Tapes by Jack Hartman

01H **How To Study The Bible** (Part 1) - 21 Scriptural reasons why it's important to study the Bible.

02H **How to Study the Bible** (Part 2) - A step-by-step, detailed explanation of a proven, effective system for studying the Bible.

03H **Enter Into God's Rest** - Don't struggle with loads that are too heavy for you. Learn exactly what God's Word teaches about relaxing under pressure.

04H **Freedom From Worry** - A comprehensive Scriptural explanation on how to become completely free from worry.

05H **God's Strength, Our Weakness** - God's strength is available to the degree that we can admit our human weakness and trust instead in His unlimited strength.

06H **How To Transform Our Lives** - A thorough, Scriptural study of how we can change our lives completely through a spiritual renewal of our minds.

07H **The Greatest Power in the Universe** (Part 1) - The greatest power in the universe is love. This tape gives a beautiful Scriptural explanation of our Father's love for us.

08H **The Greatest Power in the Universe** (Part 2) - A thorough Scriptural explanation of our love for God and for each other, as well as how to overcome fear through love.

09H **How Well Do You Know Jesus Christ?** - An Easter Sunday message that received great audience response. After this message, you'll know Jesus as you never knew Him before.

10H **God's Perfect Peace** - In a world of unrest, people everywhere are searching for inner peace. This is a detailed Scriptural explanation of how to obtain God's perfect peace.

11H **Freedom Through Surrender** - Millions of people are trying to find freedom by "doing their own thing." God's Word tells us to do just the opposite. Freedom comes only as a result of daily surrender of our lives to Jesus Christ.

12H **Overcoming Anger** - Do you know when anger is permissible and when it is a sin? Learn step-by-step procedures from the Bible on how to overcome the sinful effects of anger.

13H **Taking Possession of Our Souls** - God's Word teaches that patience is the key to the possession of our souls. Learn why God allows us to have severe problems, why He sometimes makes us wait for His answer, and how to increase patience and endurance.

14H **Staying Young in the Lord** - Our generation tries to cover up the aging process with makeup, hair coloring, hair pieces, etc. The Bible teaches us a better way. Learn specific, factual methods to offset the aging process.

15H **Two Different Worlds** - A specific explanation of how to enter into the spiritual realm in order to learn the great truths our Father wants to reveal to us.

16H **Trust God For Your Finances** - In response to many requests, this tape contains a summary of the highlights of Jack's best-selling book "Trust God For Your Finances."

17H **The Joy of the Lord** - How can Christians experience the joy of the Lord regardless of the external circumstances they may be faced with? More than 50 Scriptural references are used to answer this question.

18H **Let Go and Let God** - Most Christians know the Word of God tells us to let go of our problems and give them to the Lord. However, this is easier said than done. This message tells us how to give our problems to the Lord and leave them with Him.

19H **Guidance, Power, Comfort and Wisdom** - Learn how to receive the blessings available to Christians from the Holy Spirit Who lives within us to guide us, empower us, comfort us, and give us wisdom.

20H **Go With God** - In this tape, Jack carefully outlines 35 Scripture references to explain why and how we as Christians should witness to the unsaved.

21H **One Day at a Time** - In this tape, Jack points out that we are neither to dwell on the past nor worry about the future. He emphasizes Jesus' specific instructions to live our lives in "day tight" compartments, forgetting the past and leaving the future in His hands.

22H **Never, Never Give Up** - Our Father wants our faith, but He often requires more than this. Sometimes we need endurance and perseverance as well. Jesus Christ has given us the victory, but we must not give up until this victory is brought into manifestation in our lives.

23H **The Christ-Centered Life** - Too many of us are still on the throne of our lives doing what we want to do and pursuing personal goals. Jesus Christ lives in us and He wants to live His life through us. This tape shows us how to allow Him to do this.

24H **Fear Must Disappear** - The spirit of fear cannot stand up against perfect love. When we resist Satan through perfect love, the spirit of fear must flee. What is perfect love and how do we attain it? Listen to this tape and find out.

25H **Internal Security** - Some Christians fall into the same trap the world does: looking for security from external sources. In this tape, Jack shares his belief that difficult times are ahead of us and the only security in these times will be from the Spirit of God and the Word of God living in our hearts.

26H **Continually Increasing Faith** - Romans 12:3 tells us that all Christians start out with a specific amount of faith. In these last days before Jesus returns, we will all need a stronger faith than just the minimum. This tape offers many specific suggestions on what to do to continually strengthen our faith.

27H **Why Does God Allow Adversity?** - Several Scriptural references are used in this tape to explain the development of strong faith through adversity.

28H **Faith Works By Love** - Galatians 5:6 tells us that faith works by love. Christians wondering why their faith doesn't seem to be working may find an answer in this message. A life centered around the love of the Lord for us and our love for others is absolutely necessary to strong faith.

29H **There Are No Hopeless Situations** - Satan wants us to feel hopeless. He wants us to give up hope and quit. This tape explains the difference between hope and faith. It tells how we set our goals through hope and bring them into manifestation through strong, unwavering faith.

30H **Walk By Faith, Not By Sight** - It's very easy for even the most mature Christian to react to circumstances. When we're faced with seemingly unsolvable problems, it's easy to focus our attention on the problems instead of upon the Word of God and the Spirit of God. In this tape, Jack gives many personal examples of difficult situations in his life and how the Lord honored his faith and the faith of others who prayed for him.

31H **Stay Close To The Lord** - Many Christians hear faith principles taught, try them and then quickly give up, thinking they don't work. Our faith is only as strong as its source. A close relationship with the Lord is essential to strong faith. In this tape, Jack explores God's Word to give a thorough explanation on how to develop a closer relationship with the Lord.

32H **Quiet Faith** - Sometimes when we're faced with very difficult problems, the hardest thing to do is to be still. The Holy Spirit, however, never reacts to external problems and always remains calm. He wants us to refuse to be rattled and to remain quiet and calm because of our faith in Him. This message carefully examines the Word of God for an explanation on how we can do this.

33H **When Human Logic is Insufficient** - Our Father gave us our minds to think with and our hearts to believe with. Human logic and reason often miss God. This message explains why some Christians block the Lord because they're unable to bypass their intellects and place their trust completely in Him.

34H **The Good Fight of Faith** - In this message, Jack compares the "good fight of faith" with the "bad" fight of faith. He explains who we fight against, where the battle is fought, and how it is won.

Each tape is based on extensive Bible Study and contains a significant number of Scripture references and is approximately 40 minutes long.

Each tape is $4.00. However, through our quantity discount, it is possible to buy each tape for the very low price of $2.00 each! Please see the attached order form for details.

To receive additional order forms, write to:

Lamplight Ministries
P.O. Box 1307
Dunedin, FL 34697

Books/Cassette Tape Order Form

BOOK TITLE	PRICE	QT'Y	TOTAL
Increased Energy and Vitality	$9.95	_____	_____
Never, Never Give Up	$7.95	_____	_____
Strong Faith For the Last Days	$7.95	_____	_____
Trust God For Your Finances	$6.95	_____	_____
Deep Inner Peace	$6.95	_____	_____
What Will Heaven Be Like	$6.95	_____	_____
Conquering Fear	$6.95	_____	_____
Soaring Above the Problems of Life	$6.95	_____	_____
God's Will For Our Lives	$6.95	_____	_____
How To Study The Bible	$5.00	_____	_____
Nuggets of Faith	$4.00	_____	_____
100 Years From Today	$4.00	_____	_____

Cassette Tapes $4.00 @ (indicate quantity of order)

___01H	___02H	___03H	___04H	___05H	___06H	___07H
___08H	___09H	___10H	___11H	___12H	___13H	___14H
___15H	___16H	___17H	___18H	___19H	___20H	___21H
___22H	___23H	___24H	___25H	___26H	___27H	___28H
___29H	___30H	___31H	___32H	___33H	___34H	

Total Price books and tapes $_____

Minus 40% discount (5-9 items)   –$_____

or

Minus 50% discount (10 or more items)   –$_____

Net Price of Order $_____

Florida Residents only, 7% sales tax $_____

+15% before discount for postage & handling $_____

Enclosed check or money order $_____
(Please do not send cash)

Make check payable to: Lamplight Ministries
Mail order to: P.O. Box 1307
                           Dunedin, FL 34697

Name _____

Address _____

City _____

State or Province _____

Zip or Postal Code _____

Foreign orders must be submitted in U.S. dollars.

Books/Cassette Tape Order Form

BOOK TITLE	PRICE	QT'Y	TOTAL
Increased Energy and Vitality	$9.95	_____	_____
Never, Never Give Up	$7.95	_____	_____
Strong Faith For the Last Days	$7.95	_____	_____
Trust God For Your Finances	$6.95	_____	_____
Deep Inner Peace	$6.95	_____	_____
What Will Heaven Be Like	$6.95	_____	_____
Conquering Fear	$6.95	_____	_____
Soaring Above the Problems of Life	$6.95	_____	_____
God's Will For Our Lives	$6.95	_____	_____
How To Study The Bible	$5.00	_____	_____
Nuggets of Faith	$4.00	_____	_____
100 Years From Today	$4.00	_____	_____

Cassette Tapes $4.00 @ (indicate quantity of order)

___01H	___02H	___03H	___04H	___05H	___06H	___07H
___08H	___09H	___10H	___11H	___12H	___13H	___14H
___15H	___16H	___17H	___18H	___19H	___20H	___21H
___22H	___23H	___24H	___25H	___26H	___27H	___28H
___29H	___30H	___31H	___32H	___33H	___34H	

Total Price books and tapes $_____

Minus 40% discount (5-9 items)   –$_____

or

Minus 50% discount (10 or more items)   –$_____

Net Price of Order $_____

Florida Residents only, 7% sales tax $_____

+15% before discount for postage & handling $_____

Enclosed check or money order $_____
(Please do not send cash)

Make check payable to: Lamplight Ministries
Mail order to: P.O. Box 1307
            Dunedin, FL 34697

Name _____

Address _____

City _____

State or Province _____

Zip or Postal Code _____

Foreign orders must be submitted in U.S. dollars.